A Complete Defensive System

Black To Play
and Win
With 1...g6

GM Andrew Soltis

Revised 2nd Edition

C hess Dig

D1264980

ISBN: O-87568-177-8

Author: Andrew Soltis
Computer Typesetting: Elaine Smith
Cover: Elaine Smith
Proofreader: Ken Smith and Sid Pickard
Final Preparation & Diagrams: Ken Smith

Publisher: Chess Digest, Inc.®, 1601 Tantor, (P.O. Box 59029) Dallas, Texas 75229

Send the publisher $2.00 for the New Chess Guide that catalogs every chess book for general sale in the United States. You are given publishers, page counts, notation, and critical reviews. Also included is a free Chess Improvement Course for Beginners up through Master level players.

TABLE OF CONTENTS

	Page
INTRODUCTION	5

SECTION I   14
White Is A King-Pawn Player
1 e4, g6 2 d4, Bg7

Variation A 3 Nc3, c6!	17
Variation A1 4 Nf3	18
(a) 4 g3?!	18
(b) 4 Be3	20
(c) 4 h4	21
(d) 4 Bf4	21
(e) 4 Bc4	22
Variation A2 4 f4	43
Variation B 3 Nf3, c6!	51
Variation C 3 c3	56
Four "Other White Moves"	
(a) 3 h4	56
(b) 3 e5	56
(c) 3 Bc4	56
(d) 3 c4	57

SECTION II   61
White Is A Queen-Pawn Player
1 d4, g6 2 "delayed c4"
1 d4, g6 2 c4, Bg7 3 Nc3, d6 4 e4, Nc6

Variation A 5 d5	72
Variation B 5 Nge2	81
Variation C 5 Be3	89

SECTION III   **101**
Other Opening Moves By White

  A White plays **d2-d4** but does not   **102**
      follow with **c2-c4**

  B White plays the English, that   **112**
      is **c2-c4** but not **d2-d4**

  C White plays a Reti-like system or   **121**
      King's Indian Attack with **1 Nf3** or **1 g3**

  D White fianchettoes his Queen Bishop   **125**
      on his first two moves.

  E White plays a Bird's Opening **1 f4**   **138**

INTRODUCTION

To appreciate **1...g6**, consider it from the perspective of the enemy:

Of all the comprehensive opening systems for Black, none is as frustrating to play against as **1...g6**. A player with the White pieces facing a confirmed **1...g6** opponent knows that no matter what he does, he will face the same first two moves (2...Bg7). White knows he will have virtually absolute freedom for the first four or five - or more - moves and can place his center pawns and minor pieces just about anywhere on his first five ranks.

The frustration sets in when he realizes that even with that liberty White has no clear road to advantage. He gains the superior center by default. But then he spends the middlegame trying to defend it.

And depending on how he arranges those pawns, Black must have a satisfactory method of compromising the White center. Either **e4** or **d4** will inevitably become a target.

WOOD-K. ARKELL
London 1989

1 e4	c6
2 d4	d5
3 Nc3	g6
4 Nf3	Bg7

Don't be misled by Black's move order, arising out of the Caro-Kann defense. We will be examining our order of moves **1 e4, g6 2 d4, Bg7 3 Nc3** and then **3...c6** and **4...d5**, reaching the same position.

Now, in anticipation of an indirect attack on **d4** (via ...*Bg4* and ...*dxe4*) White invests in a tempo of precaution.

5 h3!	Nf6!
6 e5	Ne4
7 Bd3	

The adventures of **7 Nxe4, dxe4 8 Ng5** have so far led nowhere near a White advantage in many master game tests.

7...	Nxc3
8 bxc3	c5!

Attacking the base of the pawn chain usually pays a greater dividend in such positions than the frontal (...*f7-f6*) attack. Now with **...Qa5** coming up, White realizes his pawns are highly vulnerable. He opts for an exchange that gives him **d4** as an outpost for his pieces and good squares for his dark-squared Bishop. He is also hoping that it will cost Black.

9 dxc5	Nc6
10 Bb5	Qa5!
11 Bxc6ch	bxc6
12 Qd4?	

White preserves his extra pawn at considerable time and expense and soon finds Black in control of the b-file and several key light-colored squares.

12...	Ba6!
13 Qb4?	Qc7
14 Qd4	Rb8
15 Bf4	Rb2

White can't castle Kingside and - although legal - dare not castle Queenside. Black, meanwhile, will bring his other Rook into play in two moves and can activate his other reserve piece (the *g7*-Bishop) by way of **...f7-f6**.

16 Kd2	0-0
17 Qa4	Bc4

18 Rhb1	Rxb1
19 Rxb1	f6
20 Nd4	fxe5!

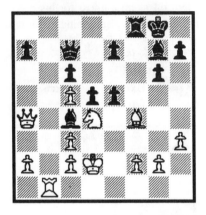

This wins two pieces for a Rook, a significant advantage in an endgame and an overwhelming edge in a middlegame with an exposed White King.

21 Ne6	Qc8
22 Nxf8	exf4
23 Nxg6	hxg6
24 Qxa7	Qe6
25 Re1	

and White resigned.

Just before **25...Bxc3ch**.

The move **1...g6** can be used in several ways. Against a King Pawn-player, it can introduce the Tseshkovsky-Gurgenidze strategy analyzed in Section I. In this case, Black builds a center with pawns at **c6** and **d5** and eventually forces a liquidation on **e4**.

If, however, White adopts a form of development that discourages this plan, Black can fall back on a Pirc Defense plan of **...d7-d6** and either **...c7-c5** or **...e7-e5**.

If White throws in **c2-c4** - whether by way **1 e4, g6 2 d4, Bg7 3 c4** or the more natural **1 d4, g6 2 c4** - then the **...d7-d5** Black move is more or less ruled out. But the advance of the c-pawn also means White lacks a natural pawn defender of **d4**. Black then directs his attention toward that square, using the **g7**-Bishop, a Knight at **c6**, the e-pawn and perhaps the **c8**-Bishop (meeting *Nf3* with *...Bg4xf3*).

FEDOROWICZ-SEIRAWAN
San Mateo 1989

1 e4	g6
2 d4	d6

Yet another move order. We'll avoid this sequence because against **3 Nc3** Black will not be able to reach our Tseshkovsky-Gurgenidze system. After White's next move, however, we transpose into an essentially Queen Pawn opening.

3 c4	Bg7
4 Nc3	Nc6!?
5 Be3	e5

This is the essence of Black's strategy: He forces White to give way at **d4**. Thanks to White's fifth move, Black cannot immediately occupy that square himself (as he would after *5 d5, Nd4!*). However, Black clarifies the center now so that he can counterattack on the wings (e.g. *...f7-f5*).

6 d5	Nce7
7 g4!?	f5

Black's interest is the Kingside and this explains White's last move. It was meant both as a warning ("Opening the Kingside with 7...f5 and you run the risk of getting mated after gxf5 and Qh5ch") and as a spacegainer (after 8 f3).

8 f3	Bh6!

Another theme of the closed center 1...g6 is that there are bound to be good Bishops and bad Bishops. White, with his eighth move, seeks to retain pawn control of key squares, such as **e4**, and keep the Kingside relatively closed. But Black's bid to trade off his "bad" dark-squared Bishop prompts White to advance his g-pawn again, thereby enabling Black to open the h-file.

By comparison, **8...f4?!** would be dubious since White could then keep the Kingside closed (9 Bf2, Nf6 10 h4, h5 11 g5 and 12 Bh3 or 9...h5 10 g5, h4! - isolating the g5-pawn - 11 c5! and White's Queenside attack is faster).

9 g5	Bg7
10 h4	h6!
11 Nh3	hxg5
12 hxg5!?	

This keeps Black's pieces constricted compared with **12 Nxg5, Nf6 13 Qd2, Nh5**. But White never manages to play **c4-c5**. The move he needs to advance his Queenside agenda.

12...	**Bd7**
13 Qb3?!	**b6**
14 a4	**a5**
15 Nb5	**Nc8!**
16 Nf2	**Rxh1**
17 Nxh1	**f4!**

This advance is as good here as it would have been wrong at move eight.

The board has been divided into two wings, with White having the superior chances on the pock-marked Queenside. But the board's only open file (along the h-line) and only open diagonal (...c8-h3) will fall into Black's hands. Moreover, the g5-pawn has been cut off from all support and must fall to Black now.

18 Bd2	**Na7**
19 Nf2	**Nxb5**
20 axb5	**Qxg5**
21 Qd1	**Rc8**

Carefully played. White had threatened **22 b4**, gaining that desperately needed open Queenside line.

22 Ke2	Nf6
23 Kd3	Qh5
24 Be2	Kf7
25 Qg1	Rh8
26 Qg2	Qh2

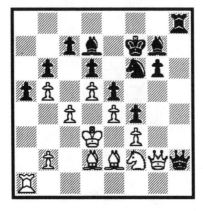

The exchange of Queens and the impending activation of Black's only bad piece (*...Bf6-h4*) produces a won endgame for Black. The game proceeds for another 26 moves (this was played in an "Active Chess" championship) but the issue is more or less decided already. White resigned on the 53rd move.

Black's strategy in this game is associated with the veteran Russian grandmaster Yuri Averbakh. Best known for his endgame books and editorship of magazines, Averbakh has introduced and refined many original ideas to opening theory and this is one of his best. In the last few years considerable effort has been made to prove a White advantage after **5 d5** - but so far Averbakh's system has stood the test of time well.

The presumptuous title, Black To Play and Win With **1...g6**, is not used to mislead you. Black is playing **1...g6** to unbalance the position - to strive for a fighting defense where the stronger player can prevail - or the weaker player, if he knows what he is about, can have winning chances from the Black side.

In the pages that follow, we analyze the various characters of 1...g6 in this order:

Section I: White is a King-Pawn Player (1 e4)
Section II: White is a Queen-Pawn Player (1 d4)
Section III: Other Opening Moves by White

SECTION I
White is a King-Pawn Player

1 e4   g6

Our defensive system will feature an attack on the center with **...c7-c6** and **...d7-d5**. Usually the Modern Defense, and its half-brother the Pirc, resembles the King's Indian Defense of **1 d4**, because Black attacks the dark squares with **...d7-d6** and **...e7-e5**, or **...c7-c5**. However, our Modern will be closer to the Caro-Kann in which it is **e4**, not **d4**, that is the target.

2 d4

By far the most logical, natural and popular response. Some players will try to avoid Pirc/Modern positions when they have White, and will tempt Black into a closed Sicilian Defense by playing **2 Nc3, 2 f4** or **2 Nf3**. Unless you are comfortable enough with those positions, you should avoid transposition to the Sicilian (*2...c5*).

One method of upsetting White's move order is **...c7-c6** a move earlier than normal, e.g. **2 f4, c6 3 Nf3, d5** and if **4 e5**, then **4...h5** as in the Gurgenidze System of Variation A2. Then White can retain strength on his central light squares **e4** and **c4** with **5 d3**. But after **5...Nh6 6 Be3, Bg4 7 Nbd2, Na6 8 h3, Nf5! 9 Bf2, Bxf3 10 Nxf3, h4** (Velimirovic-Bulat, Yugoslav Championship 1984) Black has the usual solid position he achieves in the Gurgenidze and doesn't have to "undevelop" his Bishop with ...Bf8 as he does in A2.

Black can delay or even avoid moving his c-pawn, since **2 f4, d5 3 exd5, Qxd5** is a kind of Center Counter Defense in which Black's extra move (...g6) is much more useful than White's extra move (f4). And on **3 e5, h5 4 d4, Nh6** Black has play similar to that of A2, e.g. **5 c3, c6 6 Na3, Qb6 7 Nc2, Bg4 8 Qd2, e6 9 a4, a5 10 Ne3, Nf5 11 Qf2, Be7 12 Nxf5, Bxf5 13 Nf3, Nd7 14 Be2, c5** as in **Hebden-Lobron, New York 1981.**

On the other hand, the bold bayonet of **2 h4!?** should be met by **2...h5** when both players have weakened their Kingside. This could be dangerous to Black if he allows White a direct attack on **f7** by way of **Bc4** and **Nf3-g5**, since ...h7-h6 has been taken away.

However, Black can defend by building the **c6/d5** pawn center that is the hallmark of our system. For example, **2 h4, h5 3 d4, Bg7 4 Nc3, c6 5 Nf3, d5 6 Be3, Bg4! 7 Qd2, Bxf3 8 gxf3, e6 9 0-0-0, Nd7 10 f4?!, dxe4 11 Nxe4, Qe7 (Shirazi-Soltis, Lone Pine 1979).**

On **3 Bc4** White threatens to seize the diagonal leading to **f7** before Black can contest it (3...Bg7 4 Nc3, c6 5 Qf3). But on **3 Bc4** Black should play **3...Nf6!** **4 Nc3, c6** threatening **5...d5,** e.g. **5 .e5, d5! 6 exf6, dxc4 7 fxe7, Qxe7ch 8 Nge2, Bg7 9 d3, cxd3 10 Qxd3, Bf5** with advantage to Black, or **7 Qe2 (Rigo-J. Kristiansen, Magyarorszag 1985) Nd7 8 Qxc4, Nxf6.**

2...	**Bg7**

There is no reason to tip off Black's strategy by advancing a center pawn when Black can complete the fianchetto setup with this unavoidable move. On **2...c6** White can play **3 c4!** with two points: Black cannot attack the center with ...Nc6 and White's two pawns will restrict Black's possibilities for ...d7-d5.

After **2...Bg7** we have a broad choice, to be analyzed in the following variations:

(A) **3 Nc3** retains options such as attacking in the center with **f2-f4**, or on the Kingside with **f2-f3, Be3** and **Qd2**. It also hints at Queenside castling. This is the most popular third move.

(B) **3 Nf3** begins Kingside mobilization (e.g. *Bc4* next move) and allows White to bolster his center with **c2-c3**. Less sharp than **3 Nc3**, but quite solid.

(C) **3 c3** retains aggressive intentions in the center without committing him to Nf3 or f2-f4. Other third moves such as **3 h4, 3 e5, 3 Bc4, 3 c4, 3 Be3, 3 f4** will also be covered.

Variation A
(1 e4, g6 2 d4, Bg7)

3 Nc3   **c6!**

This signals the beginning of Black's central strategy: to post his d-pawn on the fourth rank and thereby mount an indirect attack on White's d-pawn (with *...Bg4* and *...dxe4*). If White closes the center by **e4-e5**, Black will try to control the weakened light-squares such as **e4**, or undermine the enemy pawn chain with **...f7-f6**.

We now look at two main variations: **A1 4 Nf3** and **A2 4 f4**. Other fourth moves for White such as **4 g3, 4 Be3, 4 h4** and **4 Bc4** are covered in A1 notes below.

Variation A1
(1 e4, g6 2 d4, Bg7 3 Nc3, c6)

4 Nf3

Since **4...d5** is an obvious possibility, White generally declares a central strategy of his own with his fourth move.

With **4 f4** for example, he announces that he will meet **4...d5** with **5 e5**, a solid reinforced pawn chain. This is considered in the next chapter, Variaiton A2.

Or White can try to stop **4...d5** with **4 Bc4**, which we'll examine in a few paragraphs. Otherwise, Black will play **4...d5** and develop along natural lines. For example:

(a) **4 g3?!**,

has been tried by Boris Spassky, but the Kingside fianchetto is somewhat inappropriate against Black's central strategy, **4...d5**. After **5 e5, f6!**, his chain is under fire (*6 Nf3, Bg4* or *6 f4, Nh6 7 Bg2, 0-0 8 Nf3, Bg4 9 0-0, Qd7* and *...Na6-c7*). If White liquidates his chain with **5 e5, f6 6 exf6**, Black gets a fine game from **6...exf6** and *...Nh6-f7* or simply **6...Nxf6 7 Bg2, 0-0 8 Nf3, Bg4** with advantage to Black (**Sveshnikov-Tseshkovsky, Lvov 1978**) or **8 Nge2, e5 9 dxe5, Ng4 10 f4, Qb6**. The Bishop on **g2** bites on **d5** granite.

Of course if White plays **5 Bg2** instead of **5 e5**, his d-pawn comes under immediate fire after **5...dxe4!** And **5 exd5, cxd5 6 Bg2, Nf6** is the kind of game Black loves: his opponent's Queen Knight is not only misplaced in terms of its own possibilities, but it also blocks the best defense of the d-pawn, **c2-c3**.

And it makes no sense for White to play **5 exd5, cxd5 6 Bg2, Nf6** since Black has no difficulty defending **d5** and benefits more from the c-file than White does from the e-file. As usual White's **c3**-Knight then turns out to be misplaced, e.g. **7 Nce2, Nc6 8 f4?, Bf5 9 c3, b5! 10 Nf3, 0-0 11 0-0, Qb6 12 h3, b4** and Black already had the better of **Pangrazzi-Chernin, Rome 1990**.

Similar to this is **3 g3** (instead of *4 Nc3*). Then **3...d6 4 Bg2, Nc6!**, forcing the issue on **d4** after **5 Ne2, e5**. In **Karpov-Seirawan, Brussels 1992**, despite White's ability to play **c2-c4**, Black was soon equal following **6 d5, Nce7 7 c4, f5! 8 Nbc3, Nf6**.

(b) With 4 Be3,

     d5 5 Qd2 White makes provision for the defense of his d-pawn and also hints at Queenside castling. Black then has the natural developing plan of **5...dxe4 6 Nxe4, Nd7** and **7...Ngf6.** Black should be careful since this may give White too free a hand: **7 0-0-0, Ngf6 8 f3, Nxe4? 9 fxe4, Nf6 10 e5, Nd5 11 Bh6!** as in **Kupreichik-Grigorov, Lvov 1986.**

     Black may prefer to ignore the center temporarily with moves such as **5...Na6!?,** e.g. **6 0-0-0, Nc7 7 f3, b5 8 h4, h6 9 Nh3, Bxh3! 10 Rxh3, a5 11 Bd3, e6--Essegern-Baum, East Germany 1975.**

     But probably best for Black is **5...Nf6!?,** leaving White's QN misplaced. After **6 e5, Ng4 7 Bf4** Black is ready to hit back with **7...f6!,** e.g. **8 h3, fxe5 9 hxg4, exf4 10 Qxf4, Qd6!** or **8 exf6, Nxf6 9 0-0-0, 0-0 10 f3, Nbd7 11 h4, Nh5 12 Bh2, e5!** (**Teufel-Czerniak, Biel 1975** which continued *13 g4, exd4! 14 Nxd5, Ne5!*). No better is **12 Bh6, Ng3.** Notice how Black can securely recapture on **f6** in some of these positions even though he gets a temporarily backward e-pawn as a result.

     White can also reinforce his **e4** square with **4 Be3, d5 5 f3, dxe4 6 fxe4,** but this has more loosening effect than strengthening: **6...Nf6 7 Be2, 0-0 8 h3** (to avoid *...Ng4*), **Qa5 9 Qd2, c5! 10 d5, e6 11 Bf3, exd5 12 exd5, Nbd7 13 Bf4, Re8ch 14 Nge2, b5 15 d6, b4! 16 Bxa8, bxc3 17 Qxc3, Qxc3 18 bxc3, Ba6** and Black had a vicious attack in **Mukhin-Tseitlin, Tashkent 1977.**

Note that **4 Be3, d5 5 e5** will end up, after **5...h5 6 Qd2, Nh6** with play similar to our main line below except that White has not advanced his f-pawn (*7 h3, Nd7 8 Nf3, Nf8 9 Bd3, Bf5*--**Ciocaltea-Kurz, France 1975**).

(c) Unlike **h2-h4** at the second or third move, **4 h4**

can be safely ignored here: **4...d5 5 e5, h5!** after which **...Bg4** or **...Nh6-f5** can be played by Black. On **5 exd5, cxd5 6 h5** the improved situation for Black in the center makes the wing demonstration somewhat meaningless---**6...Nc6 7 Be3, Nh6! 8 Bb5, Nf5 9 Qd2, Nxe3 10 Qxe3, Bg4** as in **Kluger-Vogt, Dublin 1972**.

(d) **4 Bf4** is a bit tricky. It resembles **4 Nf3, d5 5 Bf4**, which we will examine later. After **4...d5** White can tie up Black's Queenside with **5 exd5, cxd5 6 Nb5, Na6**.

Instead, Black may do better with a normal Pirc-Defense policy such as **4..d6** followed by **5...b5** and **6...Nf6**. The White Bishop is not so well-placed on **f4** as it would be on **e3** because of the possibility of a tempo-gaining **...e7-e5**.

Play might continue (after *4 Bf4*) **4...d6 5 a4, Nf6 6 Qd2, Qa5 7 Nf3, Nbd7 8 Bc4** and now **8...e5 9 dxe5, dxe5 10 Be3, 0-0 11 0-0, Qb4** with a tiny edge for White (*Zapata-Spraggett, Novi Sad 1990*).

That leaves (**e**) **4 Bc4**:

Then Black should play **4...d6** after which **5 Qe2** or **5 Nf3** leads into "book" lines that have never shown much for White. For example, **5 Nf3, Nf6 6 e5, dxe5 7 Nxe5, 0-0 8 0-0, Nbd7 9 Bg5, Nb6 10 Bb3, Nfd5 11 Nxd5, cxd5 12 Bh4, Be6**---**Nicevski-Undovcic, Zagreb 1970** or **6 Bb3** (else *6...d5!*), **0-0 7 0-0, Bg4! 8 h3, Bxf3 9 Qxf3, Nbd7 10 Be3, e6** with a solid game.

More dangerous-looking, and what at one time was considered the "bust" to 3...c6, is **4 Bc4, d6 5 Qf3!?**, which attacks **f7** and appears to force **5...e6**. (We say "appears" because it's not clear that Black cannot gambit a pawn or two with *5...Nf6* and then *6 e5, dxe5 7 dxe5, Nd5!?*, e.g. *8 Nxd5, cxd5 9 Bxd5, 0-0*). Nevertheless, in several games in the 1960s and 1970s Black answered with **5...e6** and got a bad QB and little center activity after **...d6-d5?!**.

The right way of playing the position, however, is to safeguard **f7** and then advance the e-pawn, not the d-pawn. For example, after **5 Qf3, e6 6 Nge2** Black can continue **6...Qe7 7 Be3, Nd7** and **...e7-e5!** when White's Queen and King Knight turn out to be misplaced and Black's loss of a tempo doesn't matter much, e.g. **8 0-0-0, Ngf6 9 h4, e5** or **9 Qg3, b5**.

Black can also delay pushing any pawn to the fourth rank until he has completed his development. For example. **6...Nd7** (instead of *6...Qe7*) **7 0-0, Ngf6 8 Bb3, 0-0** and now **9 Bg5, h6 10 Bh4, Qc7 11 a4, b6! 12 Rad1, Ba6**. This is **Richagov-Eingorn, Manila 1992** which turned out well for

White after **13 Rfe1, Rae8 14 h3, e5?! 15 dxe5, dxe5 16 Ba2**, but would
have been dead even after **14...Nh7!** (instead of *14...e5*). Black won anyway.
      Better for White may be **6 Bf4!?**, offering the d-pawn in order to
castle quickly and exploit the d-file. The simple reply is **6...Qe7** and an
early **...e7-e5**. More ambitious is **6...b5 7 Bb3, a5**, which may discourage
White from placing his King on the Queenside (*8 a4, b4 9 Nce2, Qc7 10 0-
0-0, Nd7 11 h4, h6 12 Bh2, Ngf6 13 Nf4, Nb6*--not *13...e5 14 dxe5, dxe5 15
Bxf7ch!--14 Nd3, Nfd7 15 Ne2, Ba6 16 Qg3, e5* with chances for both sides,
Glek-Kantsler, Frunze 1987).

Back to our main line **4 Nf3**.

      With **4 Nf3** White believes that simple development will be suffi-
cient. the Knight is prepared to go to **e5** in some instances after that square
has been slightly weakened by **...d7-d5**.

4...   d5

As advertised. Black takes indirect aim at **d4** and directly at **e4**.

5 h3

      This is designed to stop **...Bg4**, which otherwise could pose prob-
lems for White in his defense of **d4**, e.g. **5 Be2**,

Bg4! 6 0-0?, dxe4 7 Nxe4, Bxf3 8 Bxf3, Qxd4 when White has scant compensation for his lost pawn (*9 Qe2, Nd7 10 Rd1, Qe5 11 Bd2!, Qc7 12 Nd6ch, Kf8 13 Bf4, e5 14 Be3, Ngf6*--and Black consolidates with *...Kg8* and *...Rd8*, **Treybal-Pribyl, Stary Smokovetz, 1976**).

Better is **6 Be3** with plenty of play for the pawn after **6...Nh6 7 h3, Bxf3 8 Bxf3, dxe4 9 Bxe4!, Nf5 10 Bxf5, gxf5 11 Qf3, Bxd4? 12 0-0-0!** (**Kurajica-Bulat, Yugoslav Championship 1984**). However, Black gets a fine game this time with **6...dxe4 7 Nxe4, Nd7** and **8...Ngf6** because White's Bishops are somewhat passive. There is also a promising waiting strategy of **6...e6** and **7...Ne7**.

Once Black's Queen Bishop is off the last rank, he should not fear *...e7-e6*. Another version is **5 Bd3,**

Bg4! 6 e5 when Black has no problems if he continues **6...e6!** and then
...c6-c5 (*7 h3, Bxf3 8 Qxf3, Nd7 9 0-0, Ne7 10 Ne2, c5*--**de Firmian-Dzhindzhikashvili, U.S. Championhip 1984**).

    Note however, that a trap lies in the innocent-looking move **5 Bf4.**

After **5...Bg4**, Black may find himself in hot water: **6 exd5, cxd5 7 Nb5,
Na6 8 h3, Bxf3 9 Qxf3** and not only is there no attack on **d4**---there is no
easy way for Black to develop further his Queenside pieces. One counter-
trap is **5 Bf4, dxe4 6 Nxe4, Qa5ch** and then **7 c3??, Qf5!** On **7 Nc3, Bg4!**
or **7 Qd2, Qxd2ch** or **7 Bd2, Qd5 8 Bd3, Bg4** Black has good chances.

    Next question: What happens if White, instead of wasting time on
prohylactic moves like **5 h3**, decides to resolve the center tension? Suppose

he avoids losing the d-pawn simply by moving his e-pawn at move five? The answer is that neither **5 exd5** nor **5 e5** promises much.

The former is particularly pleasant for Black. After **5 exd5, cxd5,**

Black gets a square for the development of his QN, and following **6 Bb5ch, Nc6 7 0-0, Bg4! 8 h3, Bxf3 9 Qxf3, e6** White's d-pawn is the only target in the position. Despite what you've heard about not mixing **...g7-g6** with **...e7-e6**, Black is well-protected on the dark-squares.

Typical play would then be **10 Re1, Ne7 11 Bg5, 0-0 12 Bxc6, bxc6** and in **Zakhariev-Donchev, Bulgarian Championship 1984,** Black won the endgame after **13 Bf6, Bxf6 14 Qxf6, Nf5 15 Qxd8, Rfxd8 16 Rad1, Rab8 17 b3, Rb4 18 Ne2, Rc8 19 c3, Rb6 20 b4, a5!** The superiority of Black's QN over White's was evident.

Another version of this is **5 Bd3, Bg4 6 exd5, cxd5 7 h3, Bxf3 8 Qxf3, e6 9 Ne2, Nc6 10 c3, Nge7 11 0-0, 0-0** and now **Klovan-Rytov, Leningrad 1974** saw Black playing aggressively in the center with **12 Bg5, f6!? 13 Bd2, e5 14 dxe5, fxe5 15 Qg4, Nf5** with a slight edge, although he could also have done well with the quieter Minority Attack of **...Rb8** and **...b7-b5-b4.**

And what of **5 e5**?

That also surrenders control of some key light-squares and also sets up a target for undermining. Unlike the position created by **4 f4, d5 5 e5** (discussed in Variation A2), White is not threatening a space-gaining Kingside advance here. Nor is he easily able to reinforce **e5** with his f-pawn.

Therefore, **5 e5** should be met by **5...Nh6!** and **6...f6**, e.g. **5...Nh6 6 Be2, f6 7 Bf4, Nf7 8 Qd2, 0-0 9 h3, fxe5 10 Nxe5, Nd7 11 Nxf7, Rxf7 12 Be3, e5!** (**Bellin-Gipslis, Sukhumi-Tfilis 1977**). This is an excellent illustration of the undermining strategy---Black attacks then destroys the e5-based center, then advances his own pawn to **e5**.

Similarly, **6 h3, 0-0 7 Bf4, f6 8 Qd2, Nf7 9 0-0-0** and now not **9...b5? 10 Re1, a5 11 Bd3, a4 12 a3** when Black's Queenside play is stopped (**Czerniak-Hernando, Biel 1975**) but simply **9...Na6** and **...Nc7-e6**, or **9...fxe5 10 Nxe5, Nd7**, with equalizing pressure in the center.

Usually, White will liquidate in the center when **e5** is challenged. But the open e-file that results, with a Black pawn on **f6**, is hardly dangerous for the second player.

Back to the main line after **5 h3.**

5...   Nf6

This is superior to **5...dxe4 6 Nxe4, Nf6** which leaves Black's pieces a bit misplaced by **7 Nxf6ch, Bxf6 8 Bh6!.** Black doesn't get enough counterplay from **8...c5 9 c3, cxd4 10 Nxd4, Nc6 11 Nxc6, Qxd1ch 12 Rxd1, bxc6 13 Be2, Bd7 14 Rd2, 0-0-0 15 Bc4---Tseitlin-Podgayets, U.S.S.R. Championship 1972.**

In comparable positions that we considered earlier, **5...dxe4 6 Nxe4, Nd7,** which allows Black to recapture on **f6** with a Knight, worked well. Here however, it creates problems for Black after **7 Bc4!, Ngf6 8 Nxf6ch, Nxf6 9 0-0, 0-0 10 Re1.** White's ability to attack along the e-file and use **e5** as an outpost gives him an edge, e.g.:

(a) **10...Nd5 11 c3, a5 12 a4, b6 13 Qe2, Bf5 14 Bg5, Ra7 15 Ne5, Rc7 16 Qf3, Be6 17 Bh4, Qa8 18 Bb3** and White prepares for the decisive advance of his c- and d-pawns while Black lacks counterplay (**Browne-Kovacevic, Rovinj-Zagreb 1970**).

(b) **10...b5 11 Bb3, a5 12 a4, e6 13 Ne5, Qb6 14 Bg5, Nd5 15 Bxd5!, exd5 16 Be7!, Re8 17 Bc5, Qc7 18 Ra3!, f6 19 Nxg6!** with a winning attack (**Gorshkov-Timofeyev, Krasnodar 1978**).

It is not so much the pawn structure that makes a difference here, but rather the slight difference in piece placement (Bishop on *c4*, Knight on *f6*), and this should be kept in mind.

6 e5

This is the most aggressive and most dangerous reply. It's important to compare **6 Bd3, dxe4 7 Nxe4, Nxe4 8 Bxe4, Nd7 9 0-0, 0-0** with the line in the previous note.

White's Bishop is misplaced on **e4** while Black's Knight may actually be more useful on **d7** (where it supports *...c6-c5* and keeps the White Knight off *e5*) than it would on **f6**.

Black will play **...c7-c5**, leaving White with a choice between isolating his d-pawn (*...cxd4/c3xd4*) or an exchange of pawns that will leave White with **d4** for his pieces, but will grant **c5** to Black's. Chances should be roughly equal. To illustrate, consider these possibilities:

(a) 10 c3, c5 11 Bc2, cxd4 12 Nxd4, e5?! 13 Nb5, a6 14 Nd6 (Bronstein-Tseshkovsky, U.S.S.R. Championship 1975) looks good for White, but **12...a6!** would be one improvement and **10...Qc7 11 Bg5, e6** and **12...b6, 13...Bb7**, as recommended in *Shakmatny Bulletin*, is another.

Similar to this is **10 c3, Qc7 11 Re1, c5 12 Bg5, cxd4 13 Nxd4, Nc5 14 Bc2, e5?! 15 Nb5!, Qb6 16 a4, a6 17 Qd6!** as in **Estrin-Tse-**

shkovsky, Omsk 1973. Better would have been **14...Ne6** or **14...Re8** and **...a7-a6**.

Black should time the **...cxd4** capture accurately. After **10 c3, c5 11 Bg5, h6 12 Bf4**, the movement is at hand since **12...cxd4 13 Nxd4?, e5!** wins a piece and **13 cxd4, Nf6 14 Bc2, Be6! 15 Qd2, Bd5** allows Black easy equality, **Kudrin-Dzhindzhikashvili, U.S. Championship 1984** (*16 Ne5, Rc8 17 Rfe1, Nh5 18 Bh2, e6 19 Rad1, Qg5!*). Notice that Black's Knight goes to **f6** when it is no longer needed to support **c5**.

(b) After **10 Re1** Black has several ideas. Chief among them is **10...Qc7** first, anticipating **Bf4**, and **10...Re8** followed by **11...e5**. But if Black is playing for an advantage, then **10...c5!** is his move.

Then **11 c3, cxd4 12 cxd4** (*12 Nxd4, a6* and *13...e5* or *12...Nc5 13 Bc2, e5 14 Nb5, Bd7; 14 Nb3, Qc7*), **Nf6** is typical sequence. After **13 Bc2, b6 14 Bf4, Bb7**, Black is equal (but not *13...Be6?* because of a sacrifice common to these positions--*14 Rxe6!, fxe6 15 Ng5, Qd6 16 Qe2*--**Mariotti-Tseshkovsky, Manila 1976**).

If White recaptures on **d4** with a piece rather than a pawn, Black suddenly has a Kingside majority that counts: **11...Qc7 12 Bc2, cxd4 13 Nxd4, Nc5 14 Qf3, a6 15 Bg5, e5! 16 Nb3, Ne6 17 Bf6, Nf4** with advantage to Black. (**L.D. Evans-Soltis, New York 1977**).

(c) 10 Be3 and now **10...e5** equalizes according to Larry Christiansen. For that reason **10 Bf4** is more attractive. Then Black can shift his Knight to **d5** with gain of tempo, but **10 Bf4, c5** (threatening *11...cxd4 12 Nxd4, e5*) is more thematic. After **11 d5?, Nf6** Black is better and on **11 dxc5, Nxc5 12 Bd5**, Black might grab the b-pawn or simply develop with **12...Be6**.

(d) 10 Bg5 is better than the other Bishop moves because it sets up a trap: **10...c5?! 11 dxc5!, Nxc5? 12 Qxd8** and **13 Bxe7**. However Black has a few superior methods of continuation. One is **10...Re8 11 c3, Qb6**, e.g. **12 Qd2, Nf8 13 Rad1, Be6 14 b3, Bd5** (de Firmian-Seirawan, **Wijk aan Zee 1986**).

A tricky alternative is **10...h6** and if **11 Bh4**, then **11...g5 12 Bg3, f5 13 Bd3, f4**. If instead White retreats the Bishop to **e3**, then **11...e5**, as in

(c) will lose Black's h-pawn after exchanges on **e5**. But **11 Be3** allows approximate equality from **...c6-c5**. For example, **11 Be3, c5 12 dxc5, Qc7 13 Qe2** (*13 Qd5, Nf6*), **Nxc5 14 Qc4, Ne6** or **13...Rb8!?** **14 Qb5, Nf6 15 Bd3, e5 16 Bc4, Bd7 17 Qb3, Bc6**--**Chandler-Christiansen, Thessaloniki 1984.** This appears better than **11...Qc7** which invites **12 Qc1!, Kh7 13 Bf4, Qa5 14 c3, Nf6 15 Bc2, Bf5 16 Re1** with a slight pull (**Barlov-Dzhindzhikashvili, New York 1987**).

Back to the main line after **6 e5**.

6...   **Ne4**
7 Bd3

In the early days of this variation, 1970-75, White tried to punish Black with **7 Nxe4, dxe4 8 Ng5**. It is impossible for Black to hold the advanced e-pawn. He can, however, drum up more than adequate counterplay by attacking the enemy center.

The wrong way is **8...f6**, attacking the front pawn chain, since the complications of **9 exf6, exf6 10 Nxe4, Qe7 11 Qe2, 0-0** and **12...f5** favor White (*12 Bf4!, f5 13 Nd6, Qxe2ch 14 Bxe2, Bxd4 15 0-0-0, Bf6 16 Bc4ch* and *17 Rhe1* with a clear edge, **Tseshkovsky-Rogers, World Open 1990**).

For example, **8...c5** and now:

   (a) 9 Bb5ch, Bd7! 10 Bxd7ch, Qxd7 11 c3, Nc6 12 Be3, 0-0-0! and White's center is crumbling. If White liquidates that center with **11 dxc5**, Black should have enough play with **11...Qc6 12 Qe2, Bxe5.**

   (b) 9 Bc4, 0-0 10 c3 also gains time to support the center. But Black has a terrific initiative after **10...cxd4 11 cxd4, Nc6 12 Be3, Qa5ch 13 Qd2, Qxd2ch 14 Kxd2, h6! 15 Nxe4, Rd8 16 Kc3, Bf5!** and so on. A game **Mallee-Pytel, Dortmund 1975** went **17 Ng3, Rac8 18 Nxf5, gxf5 19 Rac1, b5 20 Bxb5, Nd4ch 21 Kb4, Rb8! 22 Bxd4, Rxd4ch 23 Kc5, Bxe5 24 Rc2, Rc8ch 25 Bc6, Rd6 26 Kb5, Bxb2** and wins (see *Informant* #20).

   A recent try, **11 Qxd4**, avoids these complications and tempts Black into **11...Qxd4 12 cxd4, Nc6 13 0-0-0**. But Black does better with **11...Qc7!**, winning the e5-pawn (*12 Qxe4, Qxe5 13 Qxe5, Bxe5 14 0-0, Nc6* as in **Apicella-Webster, Oakham 1990**).

   White can play **10 e6** since Black cannot afford an exchange of pawns. But the forcing **10...f6 11 Nxe4, b5!** offers Black another sharp initiative and he has a terrific game (*12 Bxb5, Qa5ch*). In a game that gained considerable attention for this opening, **Spassky-Tseshkovsky, U.S.S.R. Cup 1974**, Black won after **12 Be2, cxd4 13 Bf3, Nc6 14 0-0, Qb6 15 Re1, Bb7 16 Bf4, Rfd8 17 a3, a5 18 Qd3, a4! 19 h4, b4** (or *19 Rab1, b4 20 b3, Ba6 21 Qd2, d3!*).

(c) **9 e6** is a better version of the last idea since **9...f6** would now lose the Exchange to **10 Nf7**. Black must play **9...Bxe6 10 Nxe6, fxe6** after which **11 dxc5** offers Black, despite appearances, excellent chances in the endgame: **11...Qxd1ch 12 Kxd1, 0-0 13 Ke2, Na6 14 Be3, Rac8 15 c3, Nxc5 16 g3, Na4 17 Bg2, Nxb2 18 Bxe4, Na4 19 Bd2, Bxc3** as in **Timoshchenko-Machulsky, Chelyabinsk 1974.**

(d) The other method of early liquidation, **9 dxc5**, is probably best met by **9...Qc7!** (*10 Nxe4, Qxe5*). Yet most games have continued **9...Qa5ch 10 Bd2, Qxc5 11 Bc3** with a little trap being set (*11...Bxe5? 12 Bxe5, Qxe5 13 Qd8ch!* and *14 Nxf7ch*). Also **11...Nd7 12 Bd4, Qd5** (*12...Qa5ch!*) allows **13 e6!** with advantage. White may do even better with **11...Nd7 12 Nxe4, Qc6 13 Qe2, Bxe5 14 0-0-0!**

Nevertheless, Black seems to be okay if he avoids all traps with **11...Nc6 12 Nxe4, Qb6 13 Bc4, 0-0!** (**Dvoretsky-Zilberstein, Tiflis 1973**) since **14 Qe2** allows **14...Nd4** and **14 f4** permits a check on **e3**.

See Illustrative game at end of this chapter (Variation A1).

(e) Finally there is **9 c3** without a preparatory move. With **9...cxd4 10 Qxd4!** (or *10 cxd4, f6 11 exf6, exf6 12 Nxe4, Qe7 13 Qe2, 0-0* with good compensation) **Nc6 11 Qxd8, Nxd8 12 Bb5ch, Nc6 13 Bf4, Bd7 14 e6, fxe6 15 Bxc6, bxc6 16 Nxe4** with a slight edge according to *New In Chess*.

Black may improve in this last line with **9...0-0**, and if **10 Nxe4**, then **10...cxd4 11 Qxd4, Qc7** or **11...Nc6**. Black can also avoid all of the analysis involving **8...c5** and play instead **8...f6!?**, as suggested in *New In Chess No. 6*. The *N.I.C.* analysis runs **9 exf6, exf6 10 Nxe4, Qe7 11 Qe2, 0-0 12 c3, Re8 13 Nc5, Qd8 14 Be3, f5** or **12 Nc5, Qd6 13 Be3** (*13 Qc4ch, Kh8 14 Be2, b6!*) **f5** etc.

Back to main line after **7 Bd3**.

7...   Nxc3

Unfortunately **7...f5 8 exf6 e.p., Nxf6** is positionally bad for Black (backward e-pawn) and **8...Nxc3?? 9 fxg7** is tactically much worse.

8 bxc3   c5

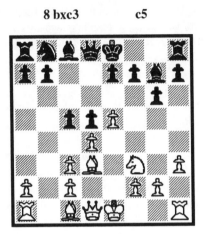

The position now vaguely resembles a Winawer Variation of the French because of the pawn structure. Black's Queen Bishop is not locked in by an **e6**-pawn as in the Winawer, and his King Bishop is still on the board. Also unlike the Winawer, Black can easily castle Kingside. And he can attack the front of the pawn chain with **...f7-f6**.

On the debit side, Black's QB lacks a good square and White can make good use of the b-file and **a3-e7** diagonal.

9 dxc5!?

At some point White probably will exchange pawns, if only to open Bishop lines, e.g. **9 0-0, Nc6 10 Re1, Qa5 11 a4, Bd7? 12 dxc5!, Qxc5 13 Rb1, b6 14 Rb5** or **13...Nd8 14 Bb5! (Sznapik-Pribyl, Warsaw 1980)**.

The exchange removes some central tension and vacates d4 at the cost of pawn security. It also avoids the constriction that can occur after **...c5-c4!?**.

For example, on **9 Bf4** Black gets good play from **9...Qa5 10 Qd2, Nd7 11 0-0, c4!** (*12 Be2, Nb6 13 Rfb1, Na4 14 Rb4, b5*--**Fedorowicz-Soltis, U.S. Championship 1977**).

Black can mix the ...c5-c4 plan with ...f7-f6, e.g. **9 0-0, 0-0 10 Re1, Qa5 11 Bd2, c4 12 Bf1, Nc6** (*12...Qa4!?*) **13 a4, f6 14 exf6, exf6, Campora-Soltis, New York Open 1987**) Or he can mix it with Queenside play: **9 0-0, Nc6 10 Re1, Qa5 11 Bd2, c4 12 Bf1, Qa4 13 Nh4, Bd7** as in **Epstein-Semyenova, Frunze 1986.**

9...   0-0

Black can try to recoup immediately with **9...Qa5 10 0-0, Qxc5 11 Be3, Qc7** but **12 Bb5ch** wins a pawn for White. In **Brooks-Lein, Lone Pine 1981**, Black obtained good compensation **12...Bd7 13 Qxd5, e6 14 Qb3, 0-0 15 Rad1, b6 16 Bd4** (*16 a4!*), **Bxb5 17 Qxb5, Nc6** because of the crippled c-pawns. He ended up getting the better game after **18 Qe2, Rfd8 19 Rfe1, Rac8 20 Qe4, Nxd4 21 cxd4, Qxc2** and eventually won.

More accurate, if Black wants to recapture on **c5** with his Queen, is **9...Nc6.** And if **10 0-0, 0-0 11 Bf4,** then **11...Qa5** is okay (e.g. *12 Qd2, Qxc5 13 Rab1*--draw agreed in **Jansa-Spiridonov, Brno 1976**).

If there is a drawback to **9...Nc6,** it is the pinning **10 Bb5.** However, **10...Qa5 11 Bxc6ch, bxc6** leaves White forced to make concessions to preserve his **c5**-pawn. After **12 Qd4, Ba6 13 Qb4, Qc7** and **14...Rb8** gives Black excellent compensation and led to a quick victory in **Wood-K. Arkell, London 1989** (see Introduction).

But, there is no particular urgency to recapturing on **c5.** And in fact, Black is better off retaking there with a Knight.

10 Be3

With this move White aims at positioning the Bishop, rather than a Knight, on **d4**. More flexible is **10 0-0**, but **10...Nd7** appears to equalize: **11 Re1, Nxc5 12 Be3, b6 13 Bf1, Bb7** and **...Rc8, ...Ne4**. Pressure along the c-file is not eliminated here by **c3-c4**, e.g. **11 Bf4, Nxc5 12 c4, Nxd3** and **13...dxc4, 14...Be6**.

10...	**Nd7**

Now on **11 0-0** Black should play **11...Qc7!**. This is more accurate than **11...Qa5** because then **12 c4** really does favor White: **12...dxc4 13 Bxc4, Nxe5? 14 Nxe5, Bxe5 15 Rb1, Bg7 16 Qf3, Qc7 17 Rb3!** with murderous play along the b-file (**Gheorghiu-Cardoso, Torremolinos 1974**).

But on **11 0-0, Qc7 12 c4, dxc4 13 Bxc4, Nxc5** chances appear in balance: **14 Rb1, b6** or **14 Qd5, Be6! 15 Qxc5, Qxc5 16 Bxc5, Bxc4 17 Rfd1, Rfc8 18 Bxe7, Be2**.

11 Bd4	**Qc7**

Black now regains material equality and the game becomes a conflict between his superior pawn structure and White's (temporary?) edge in piece activity. After **12 Qe2, Nxc5** for example, Black has no complaints, e.g. **13 0-0, b6** followed by **...Bb7** and **...Ne6** or **...Ne4**.

And in **Chandler-Gufeld, Hastings 1986-87**, Black stood very well after **12 0-0?, Nxe5 13 Nxe5, Bxe5 14 Qe2, Bh2ch 15 Kh1, e5**. White held the position following **16 Be3, e4? 17 Bb5, Be5 18 Rad1, a6 19 Ba4, Be6 20 Bb3, Rad8 21 f3, Qc6**, but **16...Bf4!** would have tested him further.

The entire variation is double-edged and dynamic---and so little explored that the best lines are not widely known. This makes it a good weapon for weekend tournaments.

ILLUSTRATIVE GAME

IGOR NOVIKOV - B. KANTSLER
Soviet Schoolboy Championship 1972

1 e4	g6
2 d4	Bg7
3 Nf3	c6

Because White can now avoid **Nc3** and play instead the more flexible **Nbd2**, some people who like Black's overall opening system, will use a different order to reach it: **1 e4, c6 2 d4, d5 3 Nc3, g6** and then **4 Nf3, Bg7**.

Of course Black then has to be ready for other Caro-Kann Defense variatons, such as **3 exd5** or **3 e5** or **2 d3**.

4 Nc3	d5
5 h3	Nf6
6 e5	Ne4
7 Nxe4	

A rare attempt to refute Black's opening. Nowadays most experienced players will develop their Bishop on **d3** at move six or seven.

7...	dxe4
8 Ng5	c5
9 dxc5	

This simplification leads to some pitfalls for Black, as noted in the earlier analysis. But there are some surprises for White too, as we discover in three moves.

9...	Qa5ch

Or **9...Qc7!?** which avoids the forcing line of play that follows.

10 Bd2	Qxc5
11 Bc3	Nd7

Avoiding the cute **11...Bxe5? 12 Bxe5, Qxe5 13 Qd8ch!** and **14 Nxf7ch.** Black's Knight move--to **d7** rather than **c6**--allows the Queen to retreat to a good square after **12 Nxe4, Qc6,** when play becomes very sharp.

12 Nxf7?

Very strong (*12...Kxf7 13 e6ch!, Kxe6 14 Bxg7*) on the face of it...

12...   0-0!

But players often forget that this optical illusion is playable. The Knight can't retreat (*13 Ng5???, Qxf2 mate*) and can't be protected. Now **13 e6** is no longer check (but *13...Bxc3* would be).

13 Qd2	**Rxf7**
14 e6	**Rxf2!**

White's position is in shambles after this clever sacrifice. the Rook must be taken since **15 exd7** is met by **15...Rxd2,** preventing the d-pawn from Queening.

Note that if Black had played **12...Rf8?** instead of **12...0-0,** White could insert **exd7** with check here.

15 Qxf2	**Bxc3ch**
16 bxc3	**Qxc3ch**
17 Ke2	

He clearly doesn't want to give up the Rook with check (*17 Qd2??*).

17...	**Qxc2ch**
18 Ke1	**Qc3ch**
19 Ke2	**Ne5!**

This stops **20 Qf7ch,** threatens the Rook and prepares to bring out the rest of the troops (*...Bxe6, ...Rd8* or *...Rf8*).

20 Qe1	**Qb2ch**

After this, the win becomes elusive. He should play **20...Qd3ch 21 Kf2, Qd4ch** and then **22...Bxe6** when the preponderance of Black attacking pieces should win.

21 Qd2!	**Qb6**

White's Queen suddenly gets back into the game now and forces a trade into the endgame. Black cannot refuse (*21...Qxa1? 22 Qd8ch* and *23 Qxe7ch*).

22 Qe3	**Qxe6**
23 Qb3!	**Kg7**
24 Qxe6	**Bxe6**
25 Ke3!	**Rd8**
26 Rc1	**Bxa2**
27 Ra1	**Bc4**

Now on **28 Rxa7** Black penetrates to the eighth rank with his Rook (*28...Rd1!*).

28 Kxe4	**Bxf1**
29 Rhxf1	**Nc4**

With three good pawns for the Exchange, Black has some winning chances. But his Knight begins to drift awkwardly here. With **29...Nc6** he centralizes better and can even afford to trade a pair of Rooks.

30 Rfc1	**Nd2ch**
31 Ke3	**Nb3**
32 Rd1	**Rxd1**

When you're down the Exchange, you generally want to keep one pair of Rooks on the board, since otherwise the enemy Rook "has no opponent" and can roam the board. Here Black might have tried **32...Ra8** and then **33...Nc5** and **34...b6**. But he feels his King has better chances of penetrating with Rooks off.

33 Rxd1	**Kf6**
34 Rd5!	

This ties down the enemy King and Knight and watches the passed a- and b-pawns. With best play, neither side can do much.

34...	a6
35 Rd7	Na5
36 Rc7	Ke6
37 Ke4	Kd6
38 Rc8	Nc6
39 Rh8	

This wins a pawn at the cost of freeing the a-pawn genie from its bottle. White can still hold---providing he keeps the Rook active.

39...	a5
40 Rxh7	a4
41 Kd3	b5
42 Rg7?	

A common error in junior chess. White wants to make sure he has his own passer and so eliminates the opposition to his h-pawn. He sees he has a King in place to stop the enemy Queenside pawns. But the momentary loss of the Rook's services allows Black's King to take the high ground.

42...	Kd5!
43 Kc2	b4
44 Rxg6	Nd4ch
45 Kb2	a3ch
46 Ka2	e5
47 h4	

Again, thinking too much about the h-pawn when activating the Rook (*47 Rg8!*) was essential, so that White can check along the files. White is now lost.

47...	e4
48 Rg3	Ne2?

But he does not lose. The correct idea was **48...Nc2!** and the advance of the e-pawn. On **49 Kb3, a2! 50 Kxa2, e3** Black's win is a matter of arithmetic (*51 Rxe3, Nxe3 52 Kb3, Kc5 53 g3, Kb5 54 h5, Ng4*, etc.)

And if White tries to make a race of it with **49 h5, Kc4 50 h6, e3 51 Rxe3** (*51 h7, b3ch*), **Nxe3 52 h7** Black calmly Queens with **52...Nc2!**

49 Re3!	**Nc1ch**
50 Kb1	**Kd4**
51 h5!	**Kxe3**
52 h6	**Draw agreed**

In contrast to the last note, Black gets nothing more than a perpetual check here: **52...Kd2 53 h7, a2ch 54 Kb2!, a1(Q)ch! 55 Kxa1, Kc2! 56 h8(Q), Nb3ch 57 Ka2, Nc1ch 58 Ka1, Nb3ch** and so on and so on.

Black should have won. See notes to game above.

Variation A2
(1 e4, g6 2 d4, Bg7 3 Nc3, c6)

4 f4

More aggressive than **4 Nf3**, this line is often selected by tactical players when they hold the White pieces---and this is one reason the positional subleties of Black's closed-center strategy often eludes them. If you're not familiar with this variation, often named after Bukhtar Gurgenidze of Soviet Georgia, the correct moves may seem very strange indeed.

4...   d5

Black can if he wants, bail out with **4...d6**, reaching a Modern Defense position that usually comes about via **3...d6 4 f4, c6**.

5 e5   h5

A move that never fails to surprise the occasional spectator. The locking of the center gives Black time for such extravagance, which is directed against White's expansion on the Kingside with **g2-g4**. If White tries to hurry the expansion with **h2-h3**, he will be punished by **...h5-h4!**

In general, Black should try to cripple the Kingside whenever possible, with that bit of pawn-play. However, even if White achieves the

Kingside expansion he seeks, the game remains difficult: **6 Be3, Nh6 7 Nf3, Bg4 8 Be2, e6 9 Qd2, Nf5 10 Bf2, Nd7 11 g3, Bf8 12 h3, Bxf3 13 Bxf3, Bb4!? 14 a3, Qa5 15 g4, hxg4 16 hxg4, Rxh1ch 17 Bxh1, Ne7**.

It would appear that Black is in retreat. But he has a dangerous source of counterplay (...*Nb6-c4!*) coming in well ahead of the White initiative (the desired *Rh1* and *f4-f5* are far away). In **Pasman-Ciocaltea, Beer Sheva 1982**, Black soon had the upper hand: **18 Bh4, Nb6 19 Rb1, Bxc3 20 Qxc3, Qxc3ch 21 bxc3, Rb8 22 Bf3, Nc4 23 a4, a5! 24 Ke2, b5 25 Bf6, Kd7 26 Kd1, Nc8** and he eventually won.

Note that Black can also play **5...Nh6** instead of **5...h5** and transpose into one of the lines below after **6 Nf3, Bg4 7 Be2, e6 8 Be3, Nf5 9 Bf2, h5**, e.g. **Chernin-Ivanov, New York Open 1988: 10 Qd3, Qa5 11 0-0, Bh6 12 g3, Nd7 13 Kg2, 0-0-0 14 Nd1, h4! 15 Nxh4, Nxh4ch 16 gxh4, Bf5 17 Qe3, Bxc2 18 Bg4, Bf8**.

Perhaps more natural for White is to meet **5...Nh6** with **6 Nf3, Bg4 7 h3** since **7...Bxf3 8 Qxf3, Qb6 9 Ne2, f6** leaves him with an edge in space that may count following **10 g4, fxe5 11 dxe5!, Na6 12 Bg2, 0-0-0 13 Be3, d4 14 Bf2** (Sveshnikov-Orlov, Pinsk 1986).

6 Nf3

This and **6 Be3** are the most common moves and they usually transpose into one another, e.g. **6 Nf3, Bg4 7 Be3, Nh6** versus **6 Be3, Nh6 7 Nf3, Bg4**.

Note that **6 Be3, Nh6 7 Qd2** is a method of avoiding the main line, but it contains the risk that after **7...Ng4** the exchange of White's bad Bishop will ultimately hurt him when the dark squares are loosened up. For example, **8 Nf3, Nxe3 9 Qxe3, Bg4 10 0-0-0, e6 11 g3, Nd7 12 h3, Bxf3 13 Qxf3** and now **13...Qb6! 14 g4, 0-0-0 15 f5, c5 16 Nb5, Kb8 17 fxe6, fxe6 18 Qf7, Bh6ch 19 Kb1, Be3!** and Black was doing well in **Savon-Gurgenidze, Gori 1971.**

6...	Bg4

6...b5 has also been tried, but it just creates more targets for White: **7 Be3, Bf5 8 Qd2, Nd7 9 g3, Nb6 10 b3, a5 11 a4!, bxa4 12 Nxa4, Nxa4 13 Rxa4--Semyenova-Khugashvili, Soviet Women's Zonal, Leningrad 1981.**

Note that after **6...Bg4** White can force matters with **7 h3, Bxf3 8 Qxf3** and he threatens **9 f5!**, liberating his Bishops and severly weakening Black's pawn structure. Once Black has committed himself to a blockade strategy with his fourth and fifth moves, he cannot afford such a situation to develop. Therefore **8...e6!** is correct.

The position then has not been tested much since the early 1970s when Fischer tried **9 g3** and got a bad game against Petrosian at the first **U.S.S.R. vs. Rest-of-the-World Match, 1970: 9...Qb6! 10 Qf2, Ne7 11 Bd3, Nd7 12 Ne2, 0-0-0 13 c3, f6 14 b3, Nf5 15 Rg1, c5 16 Bxf5, exf5**.

But if Black doesn't like these positions, he can avoid them with **6...Nh6.** And if **7 Be3,** then **7...Bg4.** Lubos Kavalek has tried a different wrinkle: **6...Nh6 7 Be3, Qb6!?** and then **8 Na4, Qa5ch 9 c3, Bg4 10 Nc5, Nd7 11 Nb3, Qc7 12 h3, Nf5 13 Bf2, Bxf3 14 Qxf3, h4 15 Bd3, e6 (Peters-Kavalek, U.S. Championship 1984).**

No better at move nine is **9...e6?!** and **10...Bf8** because Black's c8-Bishop must then emerge via the clumsy a6 route, e.g. **9...e6 10 g3, Bf8 11 Nb3, b6 12 h3, Nf5 13 Bf2, c5 14 c3, a5 15 Rg1 (Bologan-Bricard, Nimes 1991).**

But **9...Bf5!** makes sense, e.g. **10 Nc5, Qc7** with equality. (The sacrifice *10...Nd7?! 11 Nxb7, Qb6* is a bit dubious - *12 Qb3, Be4 13 Ng5, Nf5 14 Bc1* and *15 Nc5*, as in **Arnason-Hebert, New York 1989**).

7 Be3

7 Be2, e6 8 Be3 will transpose into the main line. If White avoids **Be3**, then where will he put the Bishop?

And **7 Be2, e6 8 0-0, Nh6 9 Be3, Nf5 10 Bf2**, which can transpose into lines below after **10...Bf8** or **10...Nd7**, also offers Black an opportunity here to attack the unprotected f-pawn: **10...Bh6!? 11 Qd2, Nd7 12 b4?, Nb6! 13 Nd1, Bxf3 14 Bxf3, Nc4 15 Qc1, g5!** (**Liu Wen Che-Ciocaltea, Buenos Aires 1978**).

7...   Nh6

8 Be2

More aggressive is **8 h3** with the idea of positioning the Bishop on **d3** and saving **e2** for a Knight maneuver, e.g. **8 h3, Bxf3 9 Qxf3, h4 10 Bd3, e6 11 0-0, Bf8 12 Ne2!, Nd7 13 b3, Nf5 14 Bf2, Qa5? 15 a3, b5 16 c4!** and White stands well (**Sokolov-Seret, Thessalonik 1984**).

Better is **13...Be7** or even **13...Nf5 14 Bf2, Ba3** (**Sagarin-Lyubimov, Bryansk 1985**) which denies White **c1** for his Rooks.

The idea of **...Ba3** appears in a variety of very similar lines and move orders. For instance, **8 h3, Nf5!? 9 Bf2, Bxf3 10 Qxf3, h4 11 Bd3** (by far the best square for the Bishop in this variation), **e6 12 0-0, Nd7 13 Ne2** and now **13...Bf8 14 b3, Ba3! 15 c4, Rc8 16 Rab1, a5!** (averting *17 b4* and *Rb3*) **17 Rfd1, Kf8 18 Kh2, Nb8 19 Nc3** was the final, drawn position in **Motseev-Schneider, Nettetal 1991.**

Even when White achieves **c2-c4** Black's King will find safety at **f8** or **g7**, regardless of move order. For example, **9...Nf5** (instead of *9...Bxf3*) **10 Bf2, h4 11 Bd3, e6 12 Ne2, Bf8 13 0-0, Nd7** is an alternative sequence that also leads to roughly even play following **14 b3, Be7 15 c4, Kf8!** as in **Skrobek-Kalinin, Warsaw 1989.**

Notice how these positions can be reached through different move orders. For instance, **Lanka-Gipslis, Yurmala 1983** went **8 Bd3, Nf5** (Black never fears an exchange on this square) **9 Bf2, e6 10 h3, Bxf3 11 Qxf3, h4 12 0-0, Nd7 13 Ne2, Bf8.**

Black then adopted an instructive wait-and-see strategy: **14 a4, Be7 15 a5, Kf8! 16 b3, a6 17 c4!, Rc8 18 Rfc1, Kg7 19 Kh2, Nf8 20 Be1, Rc7.** It paid off when White opened the position--**21 cxd5, Qxd5 22 Be4, Qd8 23 Bc3, Nd7 24 Bb2, Nb8 25 Qc3, Rd7 26 Rg1, Nh6 27 Raf1, Qg8 28 Qc1, Kf8 29 Rd1, Nf5 30 Bxf5, gxf5 31 Ba3, Bxa3 32 Qxa3ch, Ke8 33 Rd3, Qf8 34 b4, Rd8 35 g4, hxg3ch 36 Rdxg3, Kd7 37 d5, cxd5 38 Qa4ch, Nc6 39 b5, axb5 40 Qxb5, Rc8 41 Qxb7ch, Rc7 42 Qb6, Qb4,** etc.

8...   **Nd7**

Black has several appealing moves here: **8...e6** and **8..Nf5** among them. Play tends to be the same in both orders, e.g. **8...e6 9 Bf2, Nf5 10 g3, Bf8 11 Qd3, Nd7 12 h3, Bxf3 13 Bxf3, c5** is one typical sequence.

The Black pressure on **d4** is beginning to emerge: **14 Ne2, Qb6 15 b3, Nxd4 16 Nxd4, cxd4 17 c3, Rc8 18 Bxd4, Bc5 19 0-0, Nb8! 20 Rf2, Bxd4 21 cxd4, Nc6** and Black took over on the Queenside in **Aseyev-Titov, Kostroma 1985. 22 Rd1, Kd7! 23 Kg2, Ne7 24 g4, hxg4 25 hxg4, Rc6 26 Qe3, Qb4 27 Qd2, Qb6 28 Qe1, a6 29 Rfd2, Qb4 30 Qf2, Rc3 31 Rc2, Rxc2 32 Qxc2, Rc8 33 Qd2, Qxd2 34 Rxd2, Rc3! 35 Kf2, Kc6 36 Be2, Kb6 37 Rd3, Rc2 38 a3, Ra2 39 b4, Kc7 40 Ke3, Kd7 41 Rc3, Nc6 42**

b5? (but *42 Bf3, Na7* was also bad), **Nxd4** and White resigned. A thematic game.

Note that **8...e6 9 0-0, Bf8 10 h3!?** leads to an interesting situation in which White relinquishes, temporarily at least, his hopes for Kingside expansion. Then **10...Bxf3 11 Bxf3, Nf5 12 Bf2, h4 13 Ne2!** allows him to reorganize his pieces with **Kh2, Ng1, Be2** and **Nf3**, thereby taking aim at the **h4** pawn and also aiming at **c2-c4**. A good counter-plan, suggested by Vladimir Savon, is **...Na6-c7** and, after **...Kf8**, the shift of the Knight to **h5** via **e8** and **g7**. See also the next note.

9 Qd2

Here again the forcing **9 h3** is suspect because of **9...Bxf3 10 Bxf3, h4!**, crippling the Kingside.

Typical play would then be **11 0-0, Nf5 12 Bf2, e6 13 Ne2, Bf8 14 Kh2!, Be7 15 Ng1, Kf8! 16 Be2**. White has reorganized his minor pieces so that he can advance in the center (*c2-c4*) while keeping the Kingside in limbo. But Black should have adequate counterchances on the Queenside and center, e.g. **16...c5 17 c4, dxc4 18 d5!, exd5 19 Qxd5, Nb6 20 Qxb7, Qd5! 21 Qxd5, Nxd5 22 Bxc4, Nxf4 23 Rad1, Kg7 24 Rd7, Rhd8** (**Klovan-Podgayets, Vilna 1974**).

Because of this positional idea, it was once thought that **9 g3** was the most accurate move so that on **9...e6 10 h3, Bxf3 11 Bxf3, Nf5 12 Bf2** White will soon be ready to play **g3-g4**. However, Black can stop that plan with **9...Nf5 10 Bf2, h4!** (and *11 h3?, hxg3*). After **11 Rg1, Bf8 12 Ng5, Bxe2 13 Nxe2, hxg3 14 hxg3** Black gets his usual Queenside play from **14...c5**.

9...	e6
10 g3	

Designed to anticipate **...h5-h4**. In a similar position (Black Knight on *e7*) Gligoric has tried **10 0-0-0**, but this appears a tad too ambitious, although after **10...Qa5 11 Kb1, Nf5 12 Bf2, Bf8 13 Ne4!, Bb4 14 c3, Be7 15 Neg5** turned out all right for him---vs. Cardoso, Manila 1973.

White can throw in the move **Bf2** at various points, anticipating ...**Nf5**. For example, here **10 Bf2, Nf5** has been tried on occasion. One benefit for White is that he can reposition his **c3**-Knight with **Nd1-e3** now. But after **11 Nd1, Bf8 12 Ne3, Be7 13 g3** Black can attack the base of the pawn chain effectively (*13...c5 14 c3, cxd4 15 Nxd4!, Bxe2 16 Nexf5, gxf5 17 Ne2, Nc5! 18 Bxc5, Bxc5 19 0-0-0, Qb6* with rough equality - **Wedberg-Johansson, Stockholm 1990**). A simpler method. **12...Nxe3 13 Bxe3, Qb6 14 0-0-0, c5** also appears adequate.

10...	Bf8!
11 h3	

At an earlier point, **Bf2** might make some sense because it would anticipate **h3/...Bxf3/Bxf3/...Nf5** and ...**h5-h4**. Here, however, White has already taken the appropriate Kingside precautions. On **11 Bf2** White loses time which, even in a closed position such as this, may hurt: **11...Bb4!** and then **12 a3, Qa5!** or **12 h3, Bxf3 13 Bxf3, Nb6** with advantage to Black, e.g. **14 b3, Na4!** and **15...Qa5** or **14 0-0, Nc4 15 Qc1, Bxc3 16 bxc3,** (**Gipslis-Ubilava, Tiflis 1974**) **Qa5**.

11...	Bxf3
12 Bxf3	Nf5
13 Bf2	

13...	h4!?

Well timed. If Black waits, White will achieve **g3-g4** with a fluid Kingside mass of pawns, e.g. **13...a5? 14 Kf1, a4 15 Kg2, Qa5 16 g4!** Notice that White's alternative plan in such positions is to attack on the light squares in the center that have been weakened by **...Bxf3**, e.g. **15...Nb6 16 b3!, Bb4 17 Qd3, Kd7 18 Ne2, axb3 19 axb3, Rxa1 20 Rxa1, Qc7 21 c4!, Ra8? 22 Rxa8, Nxa8 23 cxd5, exd5 24 Bxh5!** and wins, **Marjanovic-Cioclatea, Istanbul 1980.**

It makes some sense for Black to complete his development and castle Queenside, such as with **13...Qa5.** For example, **14 g4, hxg4 15 hxg4, Rxh1ch 16 Bxh1, Nh6 17 Bf3, Nb6** and if White stops **...Nc4** with **18 b3,** he allows **18...Bb4.** A better plan for White is **14 Ne2** after which Black may do best to avoid the endgame, e.g. **14...Bb4 15 c3, Be7 16 Kf1, 0-0-0 17 Kg2, Rdg8** (preparing *18...g5*) **18 g4, Nh6!** as in **Gobet-Szmetan, Biel 1982.**

The major alternative for Black to our **13...h4!?** is the counterplay offered in the center from a quick **...c6-c5.** For example, **13...Be7 14 Nd1, Qb6 15 c3, c5 16 Ne3, cxd4 17 Nxf5, gxf5 18 Bxd4, Bc5** and now **19 0-0-0!, Bxd4 20 cxd4, Rc8ch 21 Kb1, Rc4 22 Rhg1, Nb8! 23 g4!** remains sharp---(**Mestel-Wedberg, European Junior Championship 1974**).

The chief advantage of **13...h4!?** is that it's forcing nature enables Black to meet **14 g4** with **14...Ng3! 15 Rg1, Qb6** when Black's prospects on the dark squares should offset the loss of a pawn due to the paratrooper Knight on **g3.**

In **Arnason-Christiansesn, Reykjavik 1986,** White did not take the offered pawn immediately---after all the Knight is trapped on **g3**---but played **16 0-0-0, Qa6** and then saw **...b7-b5-b4, ...Nb6-c4** coming. He continued **17 Qd3,** but Black had a safe endgame following **17...Qxd3 18 Rxd3, c5! 19 Nb5, c4 20 Rdd1, Rc8! 21 Bxg3, hxg3 22 Rxg3, a6 23 Nc3, b5 24 Rh1, Rh4 25 Ne2, Nb6 26 g5, c3! 27 b3,** (*27 Nxc3, Rxf4; 27 bxc3, Na4*) **a5.**

Black actually ended up winning after **28 Bg4, Bb4 29 Ng1, a4 30 Rh2, Ke7 31 Kd1, Ra8 32 Nf3, Rhh8 33 Ne1, Nd7 34 Nd3, axb3 35 cxb3, Ba5 36 Nc1, Nb8 37 a3, Bb6 38 Ra2, Rc8 39 Rd3, Nc6 40 Rc3, Bd4 41 Rd3, Bb6 42 b4, Nxb4 43 axb4, Rxc1ch 44 Kxc1, Ra2.**

Variation B
(1 e4, g6 2 d4, Bg7)

3 Nf3

This is a much more conservative move than its chief rival, **3 Nc3**. When White brings out his QN on the third move, he may be thinking of Queenside castling and aggressive mating attack with **Qd2** and **Bh6**. Or he can envision sharp central action with **f2-f4**. Or he may have **g2-g3** and **Bg2** in mind. But with **3 Nf3**, White is somewhat limited to conservative plans involving Kingside castling and simple piece development (*Bc4* or *Be2*, *Re1, Qe2*, etc.)

3...   c6

There is some reason (further into the variation) for Black to change from his earlier strategy, since White's center can now be reinforced with **c2-c3** and since an exchange of pawns on **d5** will not leave him with a misplaced QN. Nevertheless, we will adopt a consistent central policy.

4 Nbd2

A majority of that minority of players who use **3 Nf3**, do it with the idea of **3...d6 4 Bc4**. Here however, they discover that **4 Bc4?** is clearly wrong--**4...d5!** 5 exd5, cxd5 or **5 Bd3, dxe4 6 Bxe4, Nf6** and Black is better off than in similar positions from Variation A.

But **4 Bd3** is a distinct possibility because **4...d5 5 exd5, cxd5 6 h3** or **6 0-0** leads to a position usually arising out of the Caro-Kann (*1 e4, c6 2 d4, d5 3 exd5, cxd5 4 Bd3*, etc.) After **6 h3, Nc6 7 c3, Nh6 8 0-0, 0-0 9 Re1, Bf5** Black completes development smoothly.

Note however that with **Nf3** already played, it is hard for White to advance his e-pawn and maintain it on the fifth rank. After **4 Bd3, d5 5 e5** Black gets plenty of counterplay from attacking the front of the pawn chain with **...Bg4** and **...Nh6**, or **...f7-f6**. (But attacking the base of the chain with *5...c5* may prove less successful: *6 c3, Bg4 7 Nbd2, Nc6 8 h3!, Bd7?! 9 0-0, e6 10 Re1, Nge7? 11 dxc5!*--**Geller-Sveshnikov, Soviet Championship 1973**).

Typical of the attack on the front of the chain was **Liberzon-Hebert, Malta 1980: 4 h3, d5 5 e5, f6 6 Bf4, Nh6 7 Bd3, 0-0 8 Qd2, Nf7 9 0-0, c5!** 10 c3, Nc6 11 exf6, Bxf6 and Black was completely equal (*12 dxc5?, e5* and Black wins material). Similarly, **5...Nh6 6 c3, 0-0 7 Bd3, f6 8 0-0, fxe5 9 Nxe5, Nd7 10 Nxd7, Qxd7!? 11 Bxh6, Bxh6 12 Nd2, Qd6 13 Nf3, Qf4 (Shamkovich-Soltis, New York 1979)**.

And from yet another move order: **4 Be2, d5 5 e5, Bg4** (perhaps better than *5...Nh6* which can be answered by *6 c3, f6 7 h4* with dangers on the h-file) **6 Nbd2, e6 7 h3, Bxf3 8 Nxf3, c5!** with the better game for Black according to Ghizdavu (*9 dxc5, Nc6 10 0-0, Nge7 11 Bf4, Qa5 12 c3, Qxc5 13 Qd2, 0-0 14 Bh6, Rad8 15 Bxg7, Kxg7 16 Qf4, d4!* as in **Wolf-Ghizdavu, Rumanian Championship 1972**).

White can do better with **9 c3**, maintaining the pawn center, but then **d4** comes under attack: **9...cxd4 10 cxd4, Nc6 11 0-0, Nge7 12 Bd3, Qb6 13 b3, 0-0 14 Be3, Nb4 15 Bb1, Rac8 16 a3, Nbc6 17 Bd3, Na5 (Shamkovich-Soltis, New York 1979)**.

Finally, **4 Bf4, d5** is also OK for Black. But he may shift from a **...d7-d5** strategy to an **...e7-e5** one: **4 Bf4, d6 5 Nbd2, Nf6 6 h3, 0-0 7 Bd3, Nbd7 8 0-0, Nh5! 9 Be3, e5 10 c3, Nf4**--**Spassky-Zilberman, Spartakiade 1975**.

4...   d5

5 h3

As in Variation A1, White stops **5...Bg4**. This may not be entirely necessary since after **5 c3, Bg4 6 Bd3, Nd7 7 h3, Bxf3** White can recapture with a useful Knight, rather than a Queen. Nevertheless, the position after **8 Nxf3, dxe4 9 Bxe4, Ngf6** resembles previous positions we've examined that are good for Black when he castled and plays **...c5xd4**.

And on **5 c3, Bg4 6 exd5** Black can avoid **6...cxd5 7 Qb3** problems by retaking with his Queen.

If White omits **c2-c3**, Black can also proceed as in our main line below with **5 c3, dxe4 6 Nxe4, Nd7 7 Bc4, Ngf6**. White obtains a freer position with **8 Nxf6ch, Nxf6 9 0-0, 0-0 10 Re1**, but again with moves like **10...b6 11 Qe2, e6 12 Bf4, Bb7 (Timoshchenko-Kantsler, Frunze 1987)** Black establishes a solid game with imminent freedom from **...c6-c5**.

Another reasonable move by White is **5 Be2** when **5...dxe4? 6 Nxe4, Bg4 7 c3, Nd7 8 Nfg5!** leads to tactical problems (*8...Bxe2 9 Qxe2* and *Nd6ch* or *Nxf7!?* are coming up). Black should continue **5...Bg4** and if **6 c3**, then **6...Nd7** or **6...e6**.

But note that **5 Be2, Nf6** will reach a position similar but not quite the same as one considered in Variation A1 after **6 e5, Ne4 7 Nxe4!, dxe4 8 Ng5, c5 9 e6!, Bxe6 10 Nxe6, fxe6 11 dxc5, Nd7 12 0-0, Nxc5 13 Be3,**

Qc7 14 c3, 0-0 15 Qc2 with a slight edge (**Andersson-Mariotti, Rome 1986**).

Note also the move **5 Bd3** when **5...dxe4 6 Nxe4, Bxd4** is a questionable case of pawn-grabbing because of **7 Nxd4, Qxd4 8 Bd2** and **9 Bc3!** Black can play **5...Bg4** or **5...Nd7** instead.

5...   Nd7

Remember that **5...dxe4?! 6 Nxe4, Nd7** will allow White to post his Bishop more effectively at **c4**, and leave Black with a Knight slightly misplaced on **f6**, as mentioned in Variation A1.

6 Bd3

With **6 exd5** (or the earlier *5 exd5*) we get a kind of Caro-Kann, the Old Exchange Variation but without an early **Bf4** by White. After **6 exd5, cxd5 7 Bd3, Ngf6 8 0-0, 0-0 9 Re1, b6 10 Nf1, Bb7 11 Ng3** White has an annoying kind of pressure. Black may do better with **7...Nh6!?** followed by **...f7-f6/...Nf7** and **...e7-e5**.

At this late date White can still play **6 e5**, but he cannot maintain that point after **6...f6**. Then the exchange of e-pawns leads to a position somewhat better for White than in A1 when he had a Knight on **c3**, blocking his c-pawn. Typical play after **6 e5, f6 7 exf6, exf6 8 Bd3, Nh6 9 0-0, 0-0** would be **10 c4**.

In **Lukin-Zaichik, Beltiziy 1977** Black kept the c-file closed with **10...Nb6 11 c5, Nd7** and after **12 b4, a6 13 Nb3, Re8 14 Bd2, Nf7 15 Na5, f5! 16 a4, Nf6 17 b5, axb5 18 axb5, Qc7 19 b6, Qd7 20 Bf4, Ne4** both sides had ample chances.

6...   dxe4
7 Nxe4   Ngf6

Now **8 0-0, Nxe4 9 Bxe4, 0-0** and **...c6-c5** or **8 Nxf6ch!, Nxf6 9 0-0, 0-0 10 Re1, Qc7** (or *10...b6 11 Bf4, Bb7*) **11 Qe2, Be6 12 Ng5, Bd7 13 Bc4 (Savond-Tseshkovsky, Vilna 1975) e6!** lead to positions similar to those considered in the note to White's sixth move in Variation A1. Black's chances are good in either situation.

Variation C
(1 e4, g6 2 d4, Bg7)

3 c3

This, sometimes called the Three Pawns Attack, has faded from popularity. It retains the option of **f2-f4** with Kingside aggression in mind, or just **Nf3** with a simple scheme of development involving **Nf3, Bd3** or **Be2**, and **Nbd2**. And it stops **...c7-c5** at move three or later because after **dxc5** Black lacks the normal resources (*...Qa5ch* for example) of regaining his pawn.

Among other third moves there are:

(a) On **3 h4** Black can simply stop **4 h5** with **3...h5**, after which we get positions mentioned in the note regarding **2 h4** in the introductory section.

(b) **3 e5?!** is crude and almost never played, but it is not easily refuted. After **3...d6 4 exd6, cxd6** Black has easy development (*5 c4, Nc6; 5 Nf3, Bg4*) and if White tries to maintain the pawn at **e5**, he concedes positional liabilities (*4 f4, Nh6* or even *4...f6!?*).

(c) **3 Bc4** should be handled by **3...c6** after which **4...d5** will equalize unless White stops that advance with **4 Nc3** (transposing into Variation A1, note to White's fourth move) or **4 Qf3**, when **4...d5!? 5 exd5, Nf6 6 dxc6, Nxc6** is a gambit worthy of experimentation.

(d) **3 c4** converts the opening to a Queen Pawn, rather than King Pawn opening. Black can continue with **3..d6**, after which **4 Nc3** reaches Section II, the Modern Defense against Queen-Pawn players. However, Black can try to take advantage of White's suspicious move order by playing **3...Nc6!?** By attacking the d-pawn Black retains some clever options, since **4 d5, Nd4 5 Be3**--which is similar to a line considered in Section II-- can here be answered by **5...c5! 6 dxc6, dxc6**, after which the Knight's outpost on **d4** is maintained.

(e) Developing moves such as **3 Be3, 3 Bg5, 3 Be2** are premature since they commit White pieces to squares that may be excellent if Black plays **...d7-d6**, but not if he answers **3...c6** and **4...d5**. Either these moves will lead to positions considered earlier, or they will prove to be independent--and innocuous. For example, **3 Be3, c6 4 Qd2, d5 5 Nc3** transposes to a note to White's fourth move in A1, while **5 e5, h5** followed by **...Nh6** is similar to positions from A2.

(f) A close relative of **3 c3** is **3 f4**, also a "Three Pawns Attack", which may transpose into our main line below. By advancing his f-pawn first, White retains the option of using **c3** for a pawn or a Knight--or delaying any decision about that square, e.g. **3 f4, d6 4 Nf3, Nf6 5 Bd3, 0-0 6 0-0, Nbd7?! 7 e5!** and **Qe1-h4** with advantage to White.

The simplest and most consistent antidote to **3 f4** for our purposes is **3...d5**. This immediate advance of the d-pawn is prevented by **3 Nc3** and is dubious after **3 Nf3** (*3...d5 4 exd5, Qxd5 5 Nc3* with a good version of the Center Counter Defense). But against **3 f4** it is quite playable since **3...d5 4 exd5?!, Qxd5 5 Nf3, Bg4** points up the fact that White's third move is both time-losing and weakening.

White should meet **3...d5** with **4 e5**, then Black plays **4...Bf5** followed by **...e7-e6, ...Ne7** and the attack in the center with **...c7-c5** and **...Nc6**. The only significant game in this line appears to be **Chistyakovsky-Krementsky, Match U.S.S.R. 1968** which went **5 Ne2, e6 6 Ng3, Ne7 7 Be2, c5 8 dxc5, Qa5ch 9 c3, Qxc5 10 Nd2, Nbc6 11 Nb3, Qb6 12 Nxf5, Nxf5 13 Qd3, h5** with both Kings headed towards Queenside refuges. Perhaps better for Black is **12...gxf5!?**

Another idea is **4...Nh6** (after *3 f4, d5 4 e5*) and then **5 Bd3, Bf5** or **5 Nf3, Bg4 6 h3, Bxf3 7 Qxf3, f6** (better than *7...Nf5 8 c3* and *9 g4!* as in **Ruban-Moskalenko, Balassagyarmat 1990**).

Returning to **3 c3**...

3...   d5!

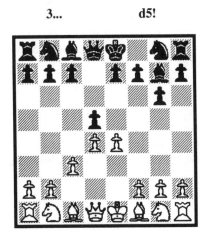

Since **c3** is occupied, Black does not tremble at the prospect of **4 exd5, Qxd5.** Black has a good alternative in **3...d6,** but the text is more forceful and restricts White's options more. Note that he doesn't need to prepare his last move with **...c7-c6.**

4 exd5

Here **4 e5, c5!** puts the White center under some pressure. After **5 Nf3, cxd4 6 cxd4, Nc6 7 Bb5, Bg4** and **...e7-e6, ...Nge7** Black stands well. White will likely prefer **5 f4, cxd4 6 cxd4,** but again **6...Nc6 7 Nc3, h5!** and **...Bg4** offers good chances (*8 Bb5, Bg4 9 Nge2, e6 10 Be3, Ne7 11 Qd2, a6* as in **Suetin-Spiridonov, Tiflis 1970**).

And if White defends **e4** with **4 Nd2,** Black can play **4...dxe4 5 Nxe4, Nd7 6 Bc4, Ndf6,** reaching a position similar to one considered in the note to Black's fifth move in Variation A2--except that Black has not wasted a tempo with his c-pawn. The little experience so far with this line has indicated Black stands well: **7 Ng5, Nd5 8 N1f3, h6 9 Ne4, Ngf6 10 Nxf6ch, exf6!? 11 0-0, 0-0** as in **Tal-Gufeld, U.S.S.R. Cup 1970.**

4...	Qxd5

Black is ready to attack the enemy center further with **5...c5.**

5 Be2

This suggestion of Pal Benko's is based on **5...Qxg2 6 Bf3**, trapping the Queen, and the fact that next move **6 Bf3** will gain time and also a nice diagonal for White.

The natural moves such as **5 Nf3** can be met by **5...c5**, e.g. **6 Be3, cxd4 7 cxd4, Nc6 8 Nc3, Qd8 9 Bb5 (Suetin-Arnaudov, Albania 1970), e6! 10 0-0, Nge7 11 d5, exd5** or **6 dxc5, Qxd1ch** (or just *6...Qxc5*) **7 Kxd1, Nf6 8 Be3, 0-0 9 Nbd2, Ng4 (Nilsson-Gaprindashvili, Goteborg 1968).**

5...	c5

Alternatives include **5...Bf5** (*6 Bf3, Be4*) and **5...Nf6.**

6 Bf3	Qe6ch
7 Ne2	cxd4
8 cxd4	Nf6

Black's Queen is a bit misplaced, but he has resolved his principle problem in the center and can begin an attack on the d-pawn. He will play ...**Rd8**, and ...**Nc6** with reasonable chances.

For example, **9 Nc3, 0-0 10 0-0, Rd8 11 d5, Qd7!** occured in **Antonov-Spiridinov, Pernik 1981** when White played **12 Nf4** to defend his d-pawn and **12...g5!** led to sharp play. The game was eventually drawn after **13 Nh5, Nxh5 14 Bxh5, g4 15 f3, Bxc3 16 bxc3, Qxd5 17 Qxd5, Rxd5 18 fxg4, Be6.**

Perhaps **11 Be3** improves for White, although **11...Nc6 12 d5, Qf5** is unclear.

SECTION II
White is a Queen-Pawn Player

1 d4	g6
2 c4	

In this section we consider positions in which White has played his c-pawn up two squares. This advance tends to discourage the **...d7-d5** plan we considered in Section I. But by denying himself the move **c4-c3** (pawns don't move backwards!), White has slightly undermined his **d4** strong point. Black, in our system, will try to exploit that with a frontal assault on **d4**. Ideally, he will occupy **d4** with his Queen Knight.

Of course White can delay **c2-c4** for a while: **2 Nf3, Bg7 3 c4**, for instance, will transpose into one of the notes to White's third or fourth moves below. But consider **2 Nf3, Bg7 3 e4, c6** (as per Section I, Variation B) and now **4 c4!?** Black could then play the position two different ways in the center. With **4...d6 5 Nc3, Bg4** he seeks to undermine the dark squares, specifically **d4**.

However, with the alternative **4...d5!?** Black confronts the enemy on the light-colored squares. So after **1 d4, g6 2 Nf3, Bg7 3 e4, c6 4 c4!?, d5**:

(a) 5 exd5, cxd5 6 c5

establishes a bridgehead that may be hard to maintain because of the attack on **d4**---**6...Nc6** and **7...Bg4**, e.g. **6...Nc6 7 Bb5, Bg4 8 Be3, e6** followed by **...Nge7-f5**.

Perhaps better is **6 Nc3, Nf6 7 Qb3** seeking a book position from the Caro-Kann. However, here White has played an extra **Nf3** in comparison with the Caro-Kann line and Black should at least equalize after **7...dxc4 8 Bxc4, 0-0 9 0-0, Nc6** threatening both the d-pawn and **...Na5**.

(b) 5 cxd5, cxd5 6 e5

denies Black's Bishop its scope, but again the attack on **d4** should equalize--
6...Nc6 7 Nc3, Nh6 8 Be2, Bg4 or **8 Bb5, 0-0 9 h3, f6**.

(c) 5 Nc3

dxe4 6 Nxe4, Nd7 (or *6...Bg4*) and **7...Ngf6** yields play similar to Seciton I,
Variation A1, except that the useful square **c4** is occupied by a White pawn
and that same pawn can no longer be used to defend **d4**.

(d) 5 e5

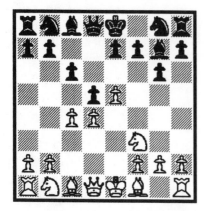

may be the most dangerous line since Black does not have the **...Nc6** counterplay he had in line (b) above. Still, after **5...Bg4 6 Nc3** and now **6...Bxf3
7 Qxf3, e6 8 Be3, a6 9 a4, Nd7 10 Bd3, Ne7** was a solid, if less than
aggressive position for Black (**Ornstein-Nicevski, Sofia 1976**). Perhaps
6...e6 is more accurate since **7 Bd3** is a doubtful pawn sacrifice
(*7...Bxf3/8...dxc4/ 9...Qxd4*) and **7 Be3, Ne7 8 h3, Bxf3 9 Qxf3, Nf5** offers
double-edged chances.

Back to the main line after **1 d4, g6 2 c4.**

2...   **Bg7**

3 Nc3

On **3 e4**, a move often played, Black can transpose into our main line below with **3...d6 4 Nc3, Nc6**. However Black has another option: **3...Nc6!?**, taking advantage of the fact that his d-pawn has not moved yet.

This is significant if White plays **4 d5, Nd4 5 Ne2** or **5 Be3** because Black can answer **5...c5! 6 dxc6 e.p., dxc6!**, a recapture impossible in Variation A below. If instead White plays **4 Nf3**, Black continues the attack on **d4** with **4...d6** (*5 Nc3, Bg4!*). And **4 Be3, d6 5 Nc3** transposes into Variation C below.

An important alternative here is **3 Nf3** followed by **4 g3, 5 Bg2** and **6 0-0**. This move order often leads into a King's Indian Defense (*3...Nf6*) and is popular because there are some K.I.D. lines in which it is better for White to delay the development of his Queen Knight until Black has declared his developmental intentions.

We will avoid the K.I.D. positions after **3 Nf3, d6 4 g3** by recommending **4...e5**. Then **5 dxe5, dxe5 6 Qxd8ch, Kxd8** yields a typical endgame that amateurs often believe to favor White (because of Black's loss of castling) when, in fact, chances are in virtual balance because of the

White weaknesses on the Queenside. After **7 Nc3, f6 8 Be3, c6** followed by **...Be6** and **...Kc7** Black has little to worry about.

Moreover, if White avoids the endgame with **5 Nc3** (instead of *5 dxe5*) Black, with **5...Bg4** overloads the **d4** square. The position after **6 d5, Ne7 7 Bg2, 0-0 8 0-0, a5** is similar to those analyzed in Variations A, B and C below, but a bit quieter. Black has not lost time with his Queen Knight and retains a variety of Kingside and Queenside plans. **Spassov-Kr. Georgiev, Bulgarian Championship 1982** was an instructive example of Black's play: **9 h3, Bd7 10 e4, Na6 11 Rb1, Qb8!** 12 Be3, c6 and now 13 Na4, Nc8 14 dxc6, bxc6 15 c5, d5 would have favored Black, but so did the game continuation, **13 b3?!, cxd5 14 Nxd5, Nxd5 15 cxd5, Bb5 16 Re1, Nb4 17 Bf1, Bxf1 18 Rxf1, Nxa2.**

Finally, some mention must be made of this move order: **3 Nf3, d6 4 e4.** This gains a tempo on our main line by avoiding **Nc3** and, incidentally, allowing White to meet **...Bg4** in some cases with **Nbd2.** Nevertheless, the situation after the thematic attack on **d4, 4...Bg4 5 Be2, Nc6** is a bit passive for White.

On **6 d5** for example, Black equalizes swiftly with **6...Bxf3 7 Bxf3, Nd4**, e.g. **8 0-0, c5 9 Na3, Nf6 10 Nc2, Nd7!?** (*10...Nxf3ch* or *10...Nxc2* are also reasonable) **11 Nxd4, cxd4 12 b3, 0-0 13 Bb2, Qb6--Najdorf-Ljubojevic, Wijk aan Zee 1972-3.**

And since **6 Ng1** can be met by **6...Bd7!**, making White's last move look silly (*7 Be3, e5 8 d5, Nd4*), the only ways for White to test Black are **6 Nbd2** and **6 Be3.** The latter demonstrates little for White after **6 Be3, e5 7 d5, Bxf3! 8 Bxf3, Nd4** because of **9 Bg4, Nf6 10 Bxd4, exd4 11 Nd2, 0-0** and **...c7-c5**, with simple equality (and not *11 Qxd4, 0-0* when both *12...Nxg4* and *12...Nxe4!* are threatened). Even worse is **7 dxe5?, dxe5** when Black virtually forces a passed pawn at **d4: 8 Qb3, Nd4 9 Bxd4, exd4 10 Nbd2, Nf6 11 Qxb7** and **Mishushkov-Foigel, U.S.S.R. 1979** went **11...d3! 12 Bxd3, 0-0 13 Qb3, Rb8 14 Qc2, Nh5** with **...Nf4** conferring a clear edge on Black.

That leaves White's best try--**6 Nbd2**--after which **6...e5 7 d5, Nce7** is highly complex after **8 Qb3, Bc8** or even **8...b6.** The latter allows **9 Nxe5, Bxe2 10 Qa4ch, b5! 11 Qxb5ch, Kf8** with great complications (*12 Nd7ch, Ke8 13 Nxb6ch?, c6!*--revealing the point of Black's 10th move--or

13 Nf6ch, Kf8 14 Nxg8, Nf5! 15 exf5, Rb8 16 Qxb8?, Qxb8 17 Kxe2, Rxg8
and Black won in **Vadasz-Adorjan, Hungary 1978**).

If these complications seem scary, Black can try **6...Nf6** (after *6 Nbd2*), threatening **7...Bxf3**. Then **7 d5, Nb8** and **8...Nbd7** will reposition his Knights more naturally than in the **6...e5** line. A game, **H. Olafsson-Speelman, Reykjavik 1990**, went **8 0-0, Nbd7 9 h3, Bxf3 10 Bxf3, 0-0 11 Re1, Re8 12 Rb1, e6 13 b3, Nc5** with even play. Speelman recommended **Qc2** at move 8 or 9.

In the last few years, the most popular sixth move for White has been **6 Be3** after which Black can plant a Knight on **d4** with **6...e5 7 d5, Bxf3 8 Bxf3, Nd4** (or *6...Bxf3 7 Bxf3, e5* etc.). When this idea arose in the **1989 Portisch-Timman** match White obtained little from **9 Bxd4, exd4 10 Na3, Ne7 11 0-0** because of **11...c6 12 Rb1, 0-0 13 Nc2, c5** and both the d-pawn and Queenside remain firm.

Instead, White has experimented with a delayed capture on **d4**, with mixed success, e.g. **9 0-0, Ne7 10 Nc3, c5 11 Bxd4, cxd4 12 Ne2, 0-0 13 b4, Qc7** (**Arlandi-Speelman, Manila 1992**).

IN GENERAL: If Black remembers how to attack **d4** with **...Nc6** and **...Bg4** or **...e7-e5**, he should have good chances in these variations.

Back to our main line after **1 d4, g6 2 c4, Bg7 3 Nc3**.

3...   d6
4 e4

This is by far the most aggressive plan, enabling White to play well-known lines of the King's Indian Defense such as the Saemisch (*5 f3*) or Four Pawn's Attack (*5 f4*) should Black now play **4...Nf6**. But our intention is to avoid K.I.D. positions and try something unusual.

There are of course, alternatives to **4 e4**. These are chiefly **4 Nf3** and **4 g3**. On **4 Nf3**, the dynamic answer is once again **4...Bg4**, undermining **d4**. This line is different from those with **4 e4**, inasmuch as White can reinforce his center here with **5 e3**. However, Canada's Duncan Suttles has shown that **5 e3, Nc6 6 Be2, e5 7 d5** (or *7 Nxe5, dxe5 8 Bxg4, exd4*), **Nce7** is not at all bad for Black.

After **8 e4, Bxf3 9 Bxf3**, the move **9...h5!?** gains important Kingside space and retains the possibility of **...Bh6**, trading off the "bad" Bishop. For example, **10 0-0, Nf6 11 Bg5, Nh7 12 Bd2, Ng8!** and in **Robatsch-Suttles, Nice 1970** Black had the upper hand after **13 Qb3?, b6 14 Qb5ch, Kf8! 15 b4, Bh6 16 Bxh6ch, Nxh6 17 c5, Ng4 18 cxd6, cxd6 19 Rac1, Kg7 20 Qe2, Ng5**. Note how quickly the Black King-attack developed (and would continue after *21 Bxg4, hxg4 22 Qxg4, Rh5 23 Qg3, Qf6 and 24...Rah8*).

In *Die Schachwoche*, IM Heinz Wirthensohn recommended **8 Qb3**, since **8...b6** allows a clever **9 Nxe5!, Bxe2 10 Qa4ch, Kf8 11 Nd7ch**. He cited **Wirthensohn-Stangl, Altensteig 1990** which went **8...Bxf3 9 Bxf3, b6 10 Qa4ch!**, leading to a positional edge, particularly in the **10...Qd7 11 Qxd7ch** and **12 e4** endgame. Perhaps best is **8...Bc8** and if **9 e4** then **9...c5**.

If White keeps the center situation fluid with **7 0-0**, Black can continue **7...exd4 8 exd4, Nge7** and a subsequent **...Nf5**, conquering **d4**, e.g. **9 Re1, 0-0 10 Be3, Nf5** or **10 d5, Bxf3! 11 Bxf3, Ne5 12 Be2, Nf5 13 Ne4, h6 14 Bd2, Qh4!** and Black stands excellently (**Podgayets-Chikovani, U.S.S.R. 1979** went *15 f4, Nd7 16 g3, Qe7 17 Bd3, Bxb2!*).

Note that White's **5 e3** avoids the doubled pawns resulting from say **5 g3, Bxf3 6 exf3**. That is not a serious pawn weakness, but Black still has an easy game with **6...c6 7 Be3, Nf6 8 f4, 0-0 9 Bg2, e6!** followed by **...d6-d5**, when the absence of his light-squared Bishop will not be missed. After **10 0-0, Nbd7 11 d5, exd5 12 cxd5, c5** Black has good counterplay and **11 Rb1, d5!? 12 c5, b5 13 b4, Ne8 14 a4, a6** (**Bagirov-Arapovic, Team Match 1985**) should equalize once Black gets **...e6-e5** in e.g. **15 Qd3, Nc7 16 Rb3, Qc8 17 Ra1, Qb7 18 Rba3, f6!**.

Back to the main line after: **1 d4, g6 2 c4, Bg7 3 Nc3, d6 4 e4**.

4...   Nc6

This is the key move to our system, popularized by former Soviet Champion Yuri Averbakh. Now that no White Pawn can protect **d4**, Black wants to overwhelm that key point in the center. Either White will concede **d4** to Black pieces or he will allow Black a favorable foothold in the center with **...e7-e5.**

The absence of **...Nf6** benefits Black in two ways. His long diagonal is not blocked, as it is for most of the opening moves of a K.I.D.. Also his King Knight is free to go to more useful squares than **f6**, such as **e7**, where it supports an advance of the f-pawn or **h6**, where it can also retreat to the strategic enclave at **f7**.

With his last move Black immediately forces White into a decision. No longer can White temporize with moves such as **5 Nf3** because **5...Bg4!** forces matters: **6 Be3, e5 7 dxe5** (*7 d5, Nd4*), **dxe5 8 Be2, Bxf3! 9 Bxf3, Nd4** and **10...c6** with a slight edge for Black. Why? Because he has an outpost in the center and White doesn't.

White may do better with **6 d5, Nd4 7 Be3**, but then **7...e5!** is fine for the second player: **8 dxe6, Nxf3ch! 9 gxf3, Bxe6** or **8 Bxd4, exd4 9 Nb5, c5** when White can't afford to grab the pawn with **10 dxc6, bxc6 11 Nbxd4** because of **11...Qb6.**

This theme of **...Bxf3** in order to establish the Knight on **d4** is common to the Averbakh system. Black should not fear the Bishops of opposite color that arise after White uses his Queen Bishop to capture the Knight on **d4**. Black's remaining Bishop is likely to be better than White's.

Having said all this, we can conclude that after **4...Nc6**, White must decide between:

(A) 5 d5, forcing matters
(B) 5 Nge2, holding the fort
(C) 5 Be3, keeping his options open

Variation A
(1 d4, g6 2 c4, Bg7 3 Nc3, d6 4 e4, Nc6)

5 d5

If this bold advance succeeds, Black's opening strategy is an instant flop. White will now try to force Black into establishing an untenable fortress on **d4** which he will later have to liquidate at great positional expense.

5...   Nd4

Yes, **5...Nb8** is legal. That is it's solitary virtue.

However **5...Ne5**, trying to provoke a series of weakening (or strengthening?) pawn advances, has also been tried. **Pergericht-Van der Wiel, Brussels 1985** went 6 h3, c6 7 Be3, Nf6 8 f4, Ned7 9 Nf3?, Nh5 10 Kf2, Nxf4! 11 Bxf4, Qb6ch! and Black was already winning.

6 Be3

This shortens Black's options to two pawn moves. There is also **6 Nge2** (not *6 Nf3?, Bg4!*) which transposes into our main line after **6...c5 7 Be3**. However, this is slightly risky for Black because White can play **7 Nxd4** instead of **7 Be3** and obtain either a small edge (after *7...Bxd4 8 Be2,*

Bg7 9 0-0, Nf6 10 Be3, 0-0 11 f4) or a big one (after *7...cxd4 8 Nb5, Qb6 9 c5, Qxc5? 10 Bd2, Qb6 11 Qa4, Bd7 12 Ba5* or *11 Rc1*).

Black can, however, play **9...dxc5** in the parenthetical variation above because he can meet **10 Bf4, Kf8 11 Bc7** with **11...Qf6 12 a4, Bd7** with a highly double-edged position in which Black's chances cannot be discounted. For example, **13 f4, g5! 14 Be5, Qh6** or **13 Qc1, b6 14 f4, Bh6** (*15 g3, Rc8 16 Qc2, Rxc7! 17 Nxc7, Bxf4! 18 gxf4, Qxf4* with excellent compensation for the Rook, as in **V. Ivanov-Losev, Central Chess Club Championship, Moscow 1990**).

What else can Black do then about **6 Nge2?** He can simply exchange pieces and play the position like a King's Indian Defense in which Black has a bit more breathing space. After **6...Nxe2 7 Bxe2** *Shakhmatny Bulletin* cites a 1962 game, **Donner-Kottnauer**, that went **7...Nf6 8 0-0, 0-0 9 Be3, Nd7 10 Qd2, Nc5 11 f3, a5 12 Rfd1** after which **12...b6** and **...e7-e5** would have equalized.

Another way of playing is to allow **c4-c5** by White and counter it with the traditional King's Indian plan of **...e7-e5** and **...f7-f5: 7...e5 8 Be3, Nf6 9 c5, 0-0 10 Rc1, Ne8 11 0-0, f5 12 exf5, gxf5 13 f4, exf4! 14 Bd4, Be5** with at least equality (**Cebalo-Nikolic, Yugoslav Championship 1986**).

The positions that arise in Variations A, B, and C in which Black plays **...N(d4)xe2** are difficult to assess. In some cases they favor White. In
- other instances they are fairly even. Generally, though, Black is doing well when he has a pawn foothold in the center, preferably **...c7-c5**, when he exchanges Knights.

6...   c5

Now **7 dxc6 e.p., Nxc6** is a Sicilian Defense of the Maroczy Bind variety, but one that is usually seen with the two Kingside Knights exchanged off. The difference appears to help Black: **8 Nf3, Nf6** (*8...Bxc3ch!? 9 bxc3, Qa5* and *10...Nf6* is a distinct alternative) **9 Be2, 0-0 10 0-0, Nd7 11 Rc1, Nc5** with good play.

7 Nge2   Qb6!

With **7...Nxe2 8 Bxe2, Nf6** Black is playing quietly for equality. The Queen move seeks complications and advantage. Note that **7...Bg4** has little point because of **8 f3**, e.g. **8...Nxe2 9 Bxe2, Bd7 10 0-0** with **f3-f4** and **e4-e5** in view.

8 Qd2

This natural defense to the attack on the b-pawn may not be best. The chief alternatives are:

(a) 8 Nxd4, cxd4 9 Na4 and now **9...Qa5ch** is the only way for Black to protect his Queen and Queen's Pawn. After **10 Bd2, Qc7**

we have a curious position in the center in which the d-pawn's presence seems to take away the best squares for White's QN and QB, at the same time that it presents White with a plan---the advance of the c-pawn.

After **11 Rc1, Nf6 12 Bd3, b6 13 b4, Ba6** Black is resisting the advance. And **11 Bd3, Nf6 12 b4** allows one of the common themes in such positions, the **...Ng4-e5** maneuver that gives Black center and Kingside counterplay: **12...Ng4! 13 Rc1, 0-0 14 0-0, Ne5 15 Nb2, a5 16 Bb1, axb4 17 Bxb4, b6** and Black has no serious problems (**Korchnoi-Speelman, Beer Sheva 1987**).

More optimistic is the immediate **11 c5** after which it is risky to try to capture and keep the pawn on **c5**, and he does better with **11...Nf6! 12 cxd6, Qxd6 13 Bd3, 0-0** and **...Ng4**, or **12 Bb5ch, Bd7 13 c6, bxc6 14 dxc6, Be6 15 Qc2, 0-0 16 0-0, d5!**, **Danailov-Brakov, Bulgaria 1984**.

White can also try to simplify the center and penetrate along the c-file with **13 Bxd7ch** (instead of *13 c6* in the last variation), **Nxd7 14 cxd6, Qxd6 15 Qb3, Qa6 16 Rc1**. This was tested in **Agnos-Webster, London (NatWest) 1990** which continued **16...0-0 17 Nc5, Nxc5 18 Rxc5, Rac8 19 Rb5**, but after **19...Rc2! 20 Qxc2, Qxb5** and **20 a4, d3!** Black had no problems.

If White is more peaceful, he can play the cowardly **10 b4** after which **10...Qxb4ch 11 Bd2, Qa3 12 Bc1, Qb4ch** is an immediate draw by repetition of moves. True, Black could avoid this by meeting **9 Na4** with **9...dxe3!? 10 Nxb6, exf2ch 11 Kxf2, axb6**. But, the soundness of this Queen sacrifice has been open to question for the last few years.

(b) 8 Na4

is a tricky version of the line above. Since **8...Qb4ch** loses immediately (*9 Bd2, Qxc4 10 Nec3, Qb4 11 Nb5!*) we concentrate on the other check. And following **8...Qa5ch 9 Bd2**, Black discovers that **9...Qc7** now allows the annoying pin **10 Bc3!**, ensuring an advantage.

For example, **10...e5 11 dxe6!, Nxe6 12 Bxg7, Nxg7 13 g3, Nf6 14 Bg2** and eventually **Nac3, Qd2** and **f2-f3** with an excellent position (**Tisdall-Davies, Oslo 1988**). Black has tried the ...e7-e5 idea with his Queen on **d8** with no better success. For example, **9...Qd8** (instead of *9...Qc7*) **10 Bc3, e5 11 dxe6, Nxe6 12 Bxg7, Nxg7 13 Qd2, Nf6 14 f3** and in **Gelfand-Azmaiparahvili, Dortmund 1990**, White even managed to preserve an edge by castling Queenside - **14...Be6 15 Nf4, Qe7 16 0-0-0!, Rd8 17 Nc3, 0-0 18 g4!.**

Therefore **9...Qa6** is forced. Then **10 Bc3, Bd7!** is harmless and **10 Nec3, Bd7 11 Bd3, Nf6 12 0-0, 0-0 13 a3?, Ng4! 14 f4, f5** can lead to good complications for Black (**Keene-Bilek, 1972**).

Better, after **9...Qa6**, is **10 Nxd4, Bxd4** (not *10...cxd4? 11 c5!*) and now:

Here White has a broad choice. In the late 1980s it was thought that **11 Nc3** was dangerous because of **11...Qb6 12 Nb5** and then **12...Bxb2 13 Rb1, Bg7 14 Qa4** with an ominous threat of **Ba5**. However, a major improvement was found in the form of **12...Bg7!** and then **13 Qa4, Bd7 14 Ba5, Qa6**, e.g. **15 Nc7ch, Kf8 16 Qa3, Bxb2! 17 Qxb2, Qxa5ch**.

White can also offer an endgame at move 12 with **12 Qb3**, e.g. **12...Qd8 13 Bd3, Bg7 14 0-0, Nf6 15 Rae1** and **16 f4** with a promising initiative (**Zsu. Polgar-Todorcevic, Pamplona 1990-91**). However, the endgame is not to be feared - **12...Qxb3! 13 axb3, Bd7** and **...f7-f5**.

Since **11 Nc3** does not actually threaten much, White may do better with **11 Be2** or **11 Bd3**. But Black should be able to hold his own on either wing. For example, **11 Be2, Nf6 12 Nc3, 0-0 13 Qc2, Bg4 14 Bd3, Bd7 15 0-0** and now **15...Ng4! 16 a4, f5** as in **Liebowitz-Fleetwood, Correspondence 1989-90** (*17 exf5, Bxf5 18 Bxf5, Rxf5 19 Nb5, Raf8!* with the main point being that *20 Nc7?* allows *20...Rxf2!*).

Similar is **11 Bd3** when **11...Bg7! 12 0-0, Bd7 13 Nc3, Qb6 14 Rb1, Nf6 15 b4** can be answered by **15...cxb4 16 a3, b3!** stifling the Queenside initiative (*17 Rxb3, Qc7 18 Nb5, Bxb5 19 Rxb5, Nd7 20 Be3, 0-0 21 a4, b6 and ...Rfc8*---**Ree-Bischoff, Plovdiv 1983**).

Getting back to **8 Qd2**...our main line:

8...   Nf6

This is based on the fact that White cannot safely capture on **d4: 9 Nxd4, cxd4 10 Bxd4?, Nxe4! 11 Bxb6, Nxd2 12 Nb5, Bf5! 13 Nc7ch, Kd7 14 Nxa8, Nxf1 15 Rxf1, Rxa8** and **16...Bxb2** or **15 Ba5, Bxb2** and Black may emerge with a material advantage.

Better for White is **10 Qxd4**, but **10...Qxb2** ends White's best Queenside chances for initiative (*11 Rb1, Qa3 12 Qd2, Qa5 13 f3, 0-0 14 Nb5, Qxd2ch 15 Kxd2, b6!* and a draw was agreed soon in **Donner-Ree, Wijk aan Zee 1972**).

9 f3

White sometimes uses the h-pawn to stop **...Ng4**, but after **9 h3** Black can simply castle with a reasonable game. On **9 h3, 0-0 10 Rd1** Black appears to get adequate counterplay from either **10...Nxe2** or **10...e5!? 11 dxe6 e.p., Nxe6** (*12 g3, Bd7 13 Bg2, Bc6* as in **Bohn-Van der Wiel, Dutch Championship 1982**).

And on **10 0-0-0**, rather than **10 Rd1,** Black gets a King-target: **10...Nxe2ch 11 Bxe2, Qa5 12 Bh6, Bxh6! 13 Qxh6, b5 14 cxb5, a6** with a stronger attack for Black (**Smith-Hergott, Kitchener 1985**).

9...   Nd7

Now however, **9...0-0** is more questionable because White can go into the line in the last paragraph (*10 0-0-0, Nxe2ch 11 Bxe2, Qa5 12 Bh6, b5 13 cxb5, a6* and use the difference in ninth moves to speed his own attack: *14 b6, Rb8 15 h4!, Qxb6 16 Bxg7, Kxg7 17 h5!* as in **Kakageldiev-Dorfman, U.S.S.R. 1979**).

10 Na4

Just as Black should not rush into castling, neither should White. After **10 0-0-0** Black can initiate a King-attack with **10...Nxe2ch 11 Bxe2, Qa5** followed by **...a7-a6** and **...b7-b5**. And if White plays **10 Rd1**, commiting himself to Kingside castling, Black can play **10...0-0** safely since **11 Nxd4, cxd4 12 Bxd4** allows **12...Bxd4 13 Qxd4, Qxb2** with typically adequate counterchances.

The exchange of dark-squared Bishops is generally OK for Black if White is left with some dark-square holes, such as **d4, c5** and **b2** in this last line.

10...   Qa6

This move, attacking the Knight, is virtually forced, but not all bad as the following sequence shows.

11 Nxd4   Qxa4
12 Nb5   0-0

And now Black appears to stand all right because of his ability to generate Queenside play with ...a7-a6 and ...Qb4. For instance, the attacking plan of **13 Bh6, Bxh6! 14 Qxh6** can be met by **14...a6 15 Nc3, Qb4 16 Qd2** (or *16 Rb1?, Ne5!*), **f5! 17 exf5, Rxf5 18 Be2, Ne5 19 b3, b5!** as in **Donner-Timman, Wijk aan Zee 1974.**

Nor does White get anything out of the endgame of **13 Be2, a6 14 b3, Qb4 15 Qxb4, cxb4.** A thematic example of this was **Savon-Nikolayevsky, Ukrainian Spartakiade 1979**:

16 Nd4, Nc5 17 Kd2, Bd7 18 Rhb1, a5 19 Bd1, Rfb8 20 a3, bxa3 21 Rxa3, b5! 22 cxb5, Bxb5 23 Rba1, Be8 (Now *24 Rxa5, Rxa5 25 Rxa5, Bxd4 26 Bxd4, Nxb3ch* is a dead draw) **24 R(1)a2, Ra6 25 Bc2, h5 26 Ne2, Rba8 27 Nc1, Bb5 28 f4, Rc8 29 Ne2, a4! 30 Bxc5, Rxc5 31 bxa4, Bc4 32 Bd3, Bxd3 33 Kxd3, f5! 34 a5, fxe4ch 35 Kxe4, Rc4ch** and Black was not worse. He eventually won after **36 Kf3, Rc5 37 Ke4, Rc4ch 38 Kf3, Rc5 39 Rd3?!, Raxa5.**

Variation B
(1 d4, g6 2 c4, Bg7 3 Nc3, d6 4 e4, Nc6)

5 Nge2

This unassuming move is seen relatively rarely nowadays because it tends to prematurely commit White to particular Kingside plans, when compared to Variation C.

5...	e5
6 d5	

Eventually White must make this advance or allow a liberating exchange on **d4**. After **6 Be3** Black can keep his options open and the center closed with **6...Nh6** (*7 f3, f5 8 d5, Ne7 9 Qd2, Nf7*). However, a simpler road to equality probably lies in **6...exd4 7 Nxd4, Nge7** with promising play based on an early **...f7-f5** or **...Ne5**. For example:

(a) 8 g3

0-0 9 Bg2, Ne5 10 b3, Bg4 11 f3, c5! 12 fxg4 (*12 Nc2, Nxf3ch!*)**, Nxg4! 13 Bg1, cxd4 14 Bxd4, Ne3! 15 Bxe3, Bxc3ch 16 Kf2, f5** and Black was going great in **Guseinov-Kantsler, Frunze 1987**.

(b) 8 Qd2

f5 9 exf5, Nxf5 10 Nxf5, Bxf5 11 Be2, 0-0 12 Bf3, Ne5 13 Be2, Qd7 (**Bragin-Zhmurov, Soviet Spartakiade 1982**). Notice that if White plays the similar **8 Be2, 0-0 9 0-0, f5 10 exf5** Black can vary from **10...Nxf5** with **10...Bxd4!? 11 Bxd4, Nxf5** when **12 Be3, Nxe3 13 fxe3, Rxf1ch** has been shown to be even in several games.

(c) 8 Be2

0-0 and now **9 Qd2, f5 10 Nxc6, bxc6 11 0-0-0** allows Black counterplay from **11...fxe4 12 g4, c5 13 h4, Rb8 14 h5, Be6 15 Bh6, Be5!**, sacrificing the Exchange (**Kalatozishbili-Chikovani, U.S.S.R. 1979**). Similarly, **10 exf5, Bxd4!** with rapid equality - **11 Bxd4, Nxf5 12 Be3, Nxe3 13 Qxe3** and **Dlugy-Seirawan, U.S. Championship 1987** was drawn here.

Better is the routine **9 0-0** after which **9...f5 10 Nxc6, bxc6** is fairly even. The exchange of dark-squared Bishops can, in fact, favor Black, e.g. **11 Bd4, Bxd4! 12 Qxd4, c5 13 Qd2, Bb7 14 Bf3, f4.** And **11 Qd2, Rb8** (*12 exf5, Nxf5 13 Bxa7, Rb7 14 Be3, Nxe3*) or just **11...fxe4 12 Nxe4, Nf5** isn't much for White.

And if White tries **9 g4** with the idea of restraining Black's f-pawn, he sets up some holes on **f4** and **h4**. After **9...Be6 10 Rg1** (*10 h4!?*), **Nxd4! 11 Bxd4, Nc6 12 Bxg7, Kxg7** the Kingside dark-square holes are exploitable. And in **Gurevich-Seirawan, U.S. Championship 1987**, they were duly exploited: **13 Qd2, Qh4! 14 Rg3?, Qxh2 15 b3, Ne5 16 Qd4, Qh1ch 17 Bf1, f6 18 0-0-0, Bxg4 19 Bg2, Qh6ch 20 Rd2, c6** and Black eventually won.

We should also mention that here as in similar positions, the entrance into an endgame - or rather a Queenless middlegame - with **6 dxe5** (instead of *6 d5*) **dxe5 7 Qxd8ch** is without energy. The loss of castling is more than made up by Black's winning of the **d4** square for his Knight (and his ability to keep a White Knight off of *d5* by playing *...c7-c6*). At least in the King's Indian and Old Indian defenses, when this early exchange of Queens is played, Black often has to delay **...Nd4**. Here he can do it fairly early in the game.

Back to the main line after **6 d5**:

6...   Nce7

This, and the comparable position with **Be3** instead of **Nge2** played by White, is a central point of controversy in the Averbakh System begun by **4...Nc6**. Is White's advantage in space more valuable than Black's counterplay along the f-file? Will Black's ability to exchange off his "bad Bishop" with **...Bh6** turn out to be positionally advantageous---or just a weakening of his King position? These questions have not been resolved in more than 20 years of grandmaster experimentation.

Note that **6...Nd4?** 7 Nxd4, exd4 8 Nb5, a6! 9 Nxd4, Qh4! gives Black some compensation for his missing pawn. But **7 Be3!** would force Black to exchange Knights in unfavorable circumstances (since *7...c5? 8 dxc6, Nxc6* leaves him with a backward d-pawn and *8...Nxe2 9 cxb7* or *9 c7* is excellent for White). The Knight exchange was not unpleasant in Variation A, when Black had played *...c7-c5* instead of *...e7-e5* and therefore had much better Queenside play and opportunities to activate his remaining Knight.

7 Ng3

Unlike the comparable position in Variation C, White cannot restrain his opponent here with **7 g4** because the pawn would simply be hanging there. He does have a choice:

(a) 7 f3,

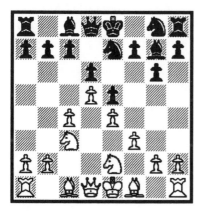

the natural idea seems to give Black a free hand after **7...f5 8 Be3, Bh6! 9 Bxh6, Nxh6 10 Qd2, Nf7**. The ability of the Knight to retreat to the excellent **f7** square, where it protects the base of the pawn chain at **d6** and avoids invading **Ng5-e6** Knights, insures equality.

After **11 g3, 0-0 12 Bg2, c6 13 0-0, cxd5 14 cxd5, Qb6ch 15 Kh1,
Bd7 16 Rae1, Kg7 17 f4, Rae8 18 Nc1** we are following **Botvinnik-
Suttles, Belgrade 1970** which favored White after **18...exf4? 19 gxf4, fxe4
20 Nxe4** but should probably favor Black a bit after **18...fxe4!.**

(b) 7 g3,

f5 8 Bg2 looks OK, but after **8...Nf6!** there is too much pressure on **e4**. If
White has to play **9 f3**, then he has nothing (*9...0-0 10 0-0, c6! 11 Kh1, cxd5
12 cxd5, Qb6* as in **Donner-Ivkov, Piatigorsky Cup 1966**).

(c) The bid for mate with **7 h4**

may turn out well if Black plays **7...h5** and makes difficult for himself the later possibilities of **...f7-f5**. This would transpose into our main line after **8 Ng3**.

But the immediate **7...f5!?** might be substituted, e.g. **8 exf5, gxf5 9 Ng3, Nf6 10 Bg5, Bd7 11 Qd2, a6 12 0-0-0, 0-0 13 h5, b5** as in **Kupper-Huebner 1978**. More dangerous would be **8 h5**.

Back to the main line after **7 Ng3**:

          7...   **h5**

Now **7...f5** may be a bit questionable after **8 exf5, Nxf5 9 Bd3** because of Black's light-square weaknesses. The text, which threatens **8...h4**, is simpler.

          8 h4   **c5**

This last move is a common one in the Averbakh. It prepares for Queenside action (*...a7-a6, ...Bd7, ...Rb8*) and also denies White the attack on the base of the pawn chain with **c4-c5**. However, it gives White another front to attack with **b2-b4**.

          9 Be2   **Bd7**

There is not sufficient reason to rush into a trade of the bad Bishop with **...Bh6**. This exchange, while generally useful, can and should be delayed until after White has spent a tempo on **Be3**. Also, there is a danger that an exchange of Bishops will allow White to open the center, say after **9...Bh6 10 Bxh6, Nxh6 11 Qd2, Bd7 12 f4!**

10 a3   Nc8

And now **11 Be3** allows **11...Bh6** with equality (or *11 Bg5, f6! 12 Bd2, Bh6* as in **Forintos-Lim, Vukovar 1976** which continued *13 b4, b6 14 b5?, Qe7 15 a4, Rb8 16 Qc2, Kd8! 17 0-0-0, a5 18 Kb2, Kc7* and Black stood slightly better).

Perhaps **11 Nf1** is better because it allows the repositioning of the Knight at **e3**, or after **b2-b4**, at **b3**. And it also meets Black's immediate threat, which was **11...Bf6** and **12...Bxh4**. Black however, can just continue his positional plans with **11...Bh6** or **11...a6** and **12...Rb8**. The positions arising then are both tactically and strategically difficult---for both players.

Variation C
(1 d4, g6 2 c4, Bg7 3 Nc3, d6 4 e4, Nc6)

5 Be3

This has recently become the most popular antidote to the Averbakh System in master chess. This Bishop will watch **c5**, a square that looms large after **...e7-e5/d4-d5**. And it allows the bayonet strategy revealed in our main line below (*5...e5 6 d5, Nce7 7 g4!?*) because the g-pawn is protected, in the absence of **Nge2**.

| 5... | e5 |

Again, our strategy is to confront White at this square. Now **6 Nge2, exd4 7 Nxd4, Nge7** will transpose into the note to White's sixth move in Variation B above.

If Black is having second thoughts, he can back out of Averbakh positions by playing **5...Nf6**, after which **6 f3** reaches a book line in the Saemisch Variation of the King's Indian.

| 6 d5 | Nce7 |

And again **6...Nd4** allows **7 Nge2** when White forces a favorable exchange of Knights.

7 g4!?

Clearly designed to restrain Black from advancing his f-pawn, this is a kind of positional "I dare you". Let's consider the alternatives:

(a) 7 Bd3

is quiet and inoffensive, and really doesn't address the problem of what to do about the coming attack on **e4**. After **7...f5** White either has to exchange pawns (*8 exf5, gxf5* when *9 f4, Ng6 10 fxe5, dxe5* or *9 f3, Bh6* are pleasant for Black) or allow the traditional Kingside advance of **8 f3, f4 9 Bf2, Nf6** and **...g6-g5-g4**, e.g. **10 Nge2, 0-0 11 c5, Rf7 12 b4, g5 13 b5, Ng6 14 c6, b6 15 a4, a5 16 bxa6, Bxa6 17 a5, bxa5 18 Rxa5, Bxd3 19 Rxa8, Qxa8 20 Qxd3, g4** with adequate play for Black, as in a Polish women's game from the 1970s.

Similarly **8 f3**

Nf6 9 Nge2, 0-0 10 0-0 and now, with White's King committed to the target zone, **10...f4** has more impact: **11 Bf2, g5 12 c5, Ng6 13 cxd6, cxd6 14 Rc1, Rf7 15 Qb3, g4 16 Nb5, gxf3 17 gxf3, Bh3 18 Rfe1, a6 19 Nc3, Nd7! 20 Kh1, Qg5** and Black won the Exchange and the game in **Geldimame-dov-Kakageldiev, Ashkhabad 1982.**

(b) 7 f4

weakens White too much on the dark squares: **7...exf4 8 Bxf4, h6!** and if **9 h4** then **9...g5!** anyway (*10 hxg5, Ng6 11 B*-moves, *hxg5* and Black has won the key *e5* square for his minor pieces).

(c) 7 Qd2

f5 8 f3 prepares for Queenside castling. After **8...Nf6 9 0-0-0** Black has a
tactical trick: **9...fxe4 10 Nxe4** (*10 fxe4, Ng4!*), **Nf5** and if White tries to
save his good Bishop with **11 Bf2??**, he allows **11...Nxe4** and **12...Bh6**.
And if he does **11 Bg5**, he will be surprised by **11...Nxe4! 12 Bxd8, Nxd2**
or **12 fxe4, Qxg5! 13 Qxg5, Bh6** when Black is slightly better because of
the bad White Bishop (*14 h4, Bxg5 15 hxg5, Ng3 16 Rh4, h5 17 gxh6, g5* -
analysis by Chikovani).

Better therefore is **8...Nf6 9 Bd3, 0-0**. Now Black gets Queenside
counterplay from **...c7-c5**, e.g. **10 0-0-0, c5 11 dxc6, bxc6 12 Bc2, fxe4 13
Bxe4, d5! and 14 cxd5, cxd5 15 Nxd5, Nexd5 16 Bxd5ch, Nxd5 17
Qxd5ch, Qxd5 18 Rxd5, e4!** with dangerous play for a pawn--**Tiller-
Karlsson, Randers 1982**.

Perhaps better is **10 Nge2** when **10...c5 11 a3** would allow White
to start a Queenside initiative aimed at **b2-b4**. But after **11...f4 12 Bf2, a6
13 b4, b6 14 Rb1, g5** chances are balanced. *E.C.O.* gives **15 bxc5, bxc5 16
h3** as best, noting a game in which **16 Qb2, g4 17 Qb6, Qd7!** turned out
badly for White.

(d) 7 c5

the immediate assault on the base of the pawn chain, which is best met by the mirror-image **7...f5**. White usually exchanges pawns here, **8 cxd6, cxd6**, and gives the disruptive **9 Bb5** check. It is generally assumed that an exchange of Bishops favors White, although this wasn't born out in a **1982 Petrosian-Ivkov** game that went **9...Bd7 10 Bxd7ch, Qxd7 11 f3, Nf6 12 Nh3, h6** and **13...0-0**.

Nevertheless, **9...Kf8** is the most interesting continuation, keeping the **f7** square free for a Knight after **10 f3, Bh6 11 Bxh6ch, Nxh6 12 Qd2, Nf7**. Now **13 f4** might be dangerous, but **13 Nge2** and other quiet moves are relatively unambitious - **13...f4 14 h4, h6 15 g3, g5 16 hxg5, hxg5 17 0-0-0, Rxh1** as in an Ivkov analysis. These lines need a lot more testing.

(e) 7 h4

seeks a quick mate, but has the disadvantage that after the thematic **7...f5 8 h5, f4!**, White's Bishop is attacked and Black has time for **9 Bd2, g5**.

True, his dark-squared Bishop is severly restricted after moves such as **10 g4**. But in a blocked position, he can reorganize his pieces at his leisure, e.g. **10 g4, Nh6 11 f3, c5 12 Nh3, Nf7 13 Nf2, Ng8! 14 a3, Nf6 15 b4, b6 16 Nd3, 0-0 17 Be2, Bd7 (Cvitan-Ivkov, Yugoslav Championship 1982)**.

Back to **7 g4**---our main line:

7...   **f5**

There is something to be said for **7...Nf6**, so that once the pawn is protected with **8 Be2**, Black can castle safely (*8...0-0 9 h4, Ne8! 10 h5, gxh5 11 Rxh5, Ng6* and *12...Nf4* according to Uhlmann). And on **8 f3** Black plays **8...Nd7 9 h4, f5 10 gxf5, gxf5** when White's eighth move has denied him the access to the Kingside via **d1-h5**.

Petursson-Speelman, Hastings 1986-7 varied slightly with **10 h5, h6 11 gxf5, gxf5** but Black again stood well after **12 Qd2, Nf6 13 0-0-0, f4 14 Bf2, b6 15 Bh4, Nh7 16 Bh3, Bf6! 17 Bxf6, Nxf6 18 Be6, Nh7.**

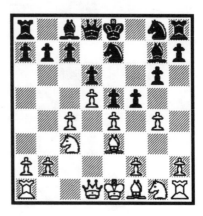

A striking position for "book". Black wants to use his spatial advantage on the Kingside. White either hopes for a mate or, more realistically, the chance to exploit the light-colored squares.

8 gxf5

This is the most testing continuation. After **8 f3** White is content to keep the Kingside in a kind of limbo, with his pawn front staking out a claim for at least equal share of the f- and g-files. He no longer has to worry about ...**f5-f4** and the ...**g6-g5-g4** roll. And if Black tries to exploit the aerated Kingside with ...**fxe4**, he may end up handing **e4** to White pieces rather than pawns, e.g. **8 f3, Nf6 9 h3, 0-0 10 Bd3, c5 11 Nge2, Bd7 12 a3, fxe4? 13 Nxe4!, Nxe4 14 Bxe4** and **h4-h5** won in **Ghitescu-Sikora, Warsaw 1979.**

But Black can force matters on the Kingside in a different way: After **8...Nf6 9 h3, h5!** White must try to blockade with **10 g5, Nd7 11 h4**, but then Black can safely castle Kingside and await Queenside events, e.g. **11...a5 12 Qd2, Nc5 13 0-0-0, b6 14 Be2, 0-0 15 Nh3, Bd7 16 Qc2, a4 17 Nf2, Qb8** and ...**c7-c6** as in **Miles-Kohlweyer, Dortmund 1986.**

In fact, if Black's aim is to lure White into pushing his g-pawn, another way of doing this is **8...Bh6**, to trade off the dark-squared "bad" Bishop (instead of *8...Nf6*). Then **9 g5, Bg7 10 h4, h6!** offers Black promising chances despite his constricted space, e.g. **11 Nh3, hxg5 12 hxg5, Bd7 13 Qb3, b6** as in **Fedorowicz-Seirawan, San Mateo 1989** (see Introduction).

8...   gxf5
9 Qh5ch

It makes some positional sense to play **9 Bh3** and exchange the light-squared Bishops. But after **9...Nf6 10 exf5, Nxf5** Black's pieces are too active and following **10 f3, 0-0 11 Qd3, Qe8!** (**Lukov-Stoikov, U.S.S.R. 1979**) Black has the easier game to play.

Nor is it attractive for White to play quietly here with **9 f3**. The opening of the g-file with **f2-f3** is a worthwhile strategy in many King's Indian variations, but with **...Ng6-f4** coming in for both attack and defense, Black should have no difficulties. After **9 f3, Nf6 10 Qd2** Black can play **10...fxe4 11 fxe4, Ng4** with excellent play.

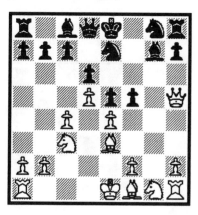

9...   Ng6!

This does not lose a piece (*10 exf5, Qh4*) and appears stronger than the older **9...Kf8** idea. After **9...Kf8** the displacement of the King is a minor concern, as demonstrated by a recent example:

Partos-Seirawan, Biel 1985 went **9...Kf8 10 exf5, Nf6 11 Qd1, Nxf5 12 Bh3, Rg8 13 Qd3, Nxe3 14 Qxe3, Bh8!** 15 Nge2, Ng4 16 Bxg4, Rxg4 17 Qh6ch, Kg8 18 b3, Bg7** and it was hard to tell that Black had not castled. He won after his Bishops took control of the Kingside---**19 Qe3, Bf5 20 Ng3, Bg6 21 0-0, Qh4 22 f3, Rxg3ch 23 hxg3, Qxg3 24 Kh1, Rf8 25 Rf2, Bh5 26 Raf1, Rf4,** etc.

No, the real problem with **9...Kf8** is **10 Bh3!, Nf6 11 Qf3** when
11...f4 leaves Black with a bad game positionally (*12 Bd2, a6 13 Bxc8,
Qxc8 14 Qd3, Rg8 15 Nf3* and *16 0-0-0* as in **Liberzon-Czerniak, Netanya
1975** or *12...c6 13 Nge2, Bxh3 14 Qxh3, Qd7 15 Qxd7, Nxd7 16 Nc1* and
Nb3). And if Black doesn't play **11...f4**, White will exchange favorably on
**f5---11...a6 12 exf5, Qe8 13 Nge2, Qh5 14 Qxh5, Nxh5 15 Bg5, Nxf5 16
Ng3** as in a 1958 game in which Averbakh, originator of this defense, gen-
eraled the White pieces.

<h3 style="text-align:center">10 exf5</h3>

The natural continuation. With Black playing his Knights to pow-
erful positions on the Kingside, White cannot dilly-dally, e.g. **10 Bh3, Nf6
11 Qf3, Nh4!**

10...   Qh4!

11 Qxh4

This is the most popular, but not necessarily productive line. In the
endgame, Black will make excellent use of the Kingside holes.

Perhaps more promising is **11 Qf3, N6e7 12 Bd3** with the idea of
meeting **12...Nh6** with **13 f6!, Bxf6 14 Ne4, Nhf5 15 Qh5ch!** as in **Ben-
jamin-McCarthy, U.S. Open 1986** (*15...Kd8 16 Nxf6* and *Bg5*). Black can
improve with **13...Rf8!** however, and then **14 Ne4, Bxf6** is quite reasonable
for Black.

Also worth a try is **12 Nb5**, rather than **12 Bd3**. Then **12...Kd8** is required and **13 Bh3, Nf6 14 Nc3, b5!? 15 cxb5, Bd7** is very double-edged. The same plan can be used against **13 Bd3**.

Finally, **11 Qf3, Nf4!?** is a gambit that has never been given much of a test.

11...	**Nxh4**
12 Nb5	

This bid for the a-pawn is the only dangerous idea at White's disposal. Following **12 Bd3, Nxf5** or **12...a6**, Black's minor pieces will be at least as good as White's.

12...	**Kd8**
13 Nxa7	

On **13 Bxa7, Bxf5 14 Be3** we transpose into the main line below. And **14 f3?** worked out very badly in **Diesen-Koshansky, Ocijek 1978** because of the simple **14...b6**, trapping the Bishop. After **15 a4, Ne7 16 a5, Kd7 17 axb6, cxb6 18 Ra3, Nc8 19 Bh3, Re8** White's predicament was obvious and he lost quickly: **20 Bxf5ch, Nxf5 21 Ne2, Re7 22 Nec3, Nd4 23 Kf2, e4 24 Ra4, e3ch 25 Kg3, Be5ch 26 Kh4, Rg7!** White resigns.

And **13 Bg5ch, Bf6 14 Bxh4, Bxh4 15 Nf3, Bf6 16 Bd3, Ne7** promises nothing either.

13...	**Bxf5**
14 Nb5	**Be4**

Other ideas here are **14...Bh6** (recommended by Haag) and **14...Nf6** (recommended by Chikovani). A recent example of the former went **14...Bh6 15 Nc3, Bxe3 16 fxe3, Nf6 17 Bh3, Be4! 18 Nxe4, Nxe4 19 Bg4? Rg8 20 h3, h5!** White resigns (**Sorosi-Arapovic, Bern 1987**) in view of **21 Bf3, Rxg1ch** or **21 Bxh5, Ng3** or **21 Bd1, Ng2ch 22 Kf1, Nxe3ch 23 Ke1, Nxd1.**

15 f3	**Bxf3!**

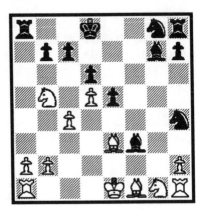

    This improvement over **15...Nxf3ch 16 Nxf3, Bxf3 17 Rg1, Bf6 18
Be2!** (Boleslavsky) makes the entire **5 Be3, e5** variation pleasant for Black.
    The endgame after **15...Bxf3!** holds no terrors any more: **16 Nxf3,
Nxf3ch** and now **17 Kf2, e4 18 Nc3, Bxc3! 19 bxc3, Ne7** favors Black's
pawn structure. Better is **17 Kd1**, but then **17...Ne7 18 Bd3, Kd7 19 Ke2,
Nd4ch 20 Nxd4, exd4** is quite equal (**Tsamryuk-Kakageldiev, U.S.S.R.
1981**).
    To repeat, if Black can establish sufficient pressure on **d4** early in
the game, he should be able to generate middlegame opportunities on one of
the two wings. Positional themes, such as exchanging off a bad Bishop with
...Bh6 followed by **...e7-e5/d4-d5**, merge with tactics, and Black must be
willing to take some risks.

SECTION III
White Plays Various Openings

So far we've concerned ourselves with orthodox opening strategies by White: He advances one of his two center pawns and he occupies as many central squares as allowed. In this section, we'll examine alternative schemes of development and priorities for the first player. They include:

(A) White plays **d2-d4** but does not follow with **c2-c4**.
(B) White plays the English, that is **c2-c4** but not **d2-d4**.
(C) White plays a Reti-like system with **1 Nf3** or **1 g3**.
(D) White fianchettoes his Queen Bishop on his first two moves.
(E) White plays a Bird's opening, **1 f4**.

In a sense, since we've decided to build our opening repertoire around **1...g6**, these alternative systems by White should not be frightening. After all, if Black with his first few moves is going to allow White to seize the center, White's refusal to do so is at least a partial acknowledgement of the soundness of Black's opening.

Nevertheless, each of these other systems packs a punch--and also denies Black one. By not putting pawns on squares where they can be attacked, White has prevented Black from his most natural source of counterplay. Often in the pages that follow, Black finds himself trying to choose between several good policies, usually predicated on which central pawn to push. But unlike Section I and II, at least here he has a choice.

Variation A
White plays d2-d4, but not c2-c4.

1 d4   g6

Now **2 Nc3, Bg7 3 e4** is a King-pawn position considered in Section I. With **2 e3, Bg7 3 Bd3** we are heading into note (a) below. And **2 f4** is a Stonewall version of Bird's Opening, Variation E.

2 Nf3   Bg7

And here **3 e4** will transpose into Section I, Variation C. However White has tried a variety of other simple developing plans in the diagram, based on putting pawns on **c3** and **e3**. He will develop one Bishop on **d3** and the other on **f4, g5** or leave it at **c1**, put the Queen at **e2** or **c2** and Rooks at **d1** and **e1**. Depending on what Black has done, a timely advance of the White e- or c-pawn can wreak havoc in the center. These innocent-looking alternative systems have borne the names of Carlos Torre and Edgar Colle, among others, and have worked well for many other fine players.

3 Bg5

Attacking the "ghost" of a Knight on **f6**. This appears to be more useful than the major alternatives:

(a) 3 e3

begins the Colle System, which scored many successes in master events of the 1920's. Those brilliancies stemmed largely from the rapid attack White developed along the **c2-h7** diagonal--a line that is curtailed by Black's first two moves.

Since there is not going to be much of an attack on **d4** now, Black answers **3 e3** with **3...Nf6** and develops normally: **4 Bd3, d5! 5 0-0, 0-0 6 Nbd2** and now **6...Nbd7** would lead, after **7 e4, dxe4 8 Nxe4, Nxe4 9 Bxe4, c5**, to a position from Section I, Variation A1 with Black being two tempi ahead (!). This is because White has taken two moves to advance his e-pawn instead of one, and Black has taken one move to advance his c-pawn, instead of two. We need not worry much about such a position for Black.

Suppose after **4...d5** White decides to revert to more normal central play with **5 c4**. Then Black has a choice between playing **5...c5**, as in an innocuous White system against the Gruenfeld Defense (*6 Nc3, cxd4 7 exd4, 0-0 8 0-0, Bg4*) or a related version of the Queen's Gambit Accepted with **5...dxc4 6 Bxc4, 0-0** and perhaps **...Bg4, ...Nc6, ...e7-e5**. In either case, Black gets a free ride in the opening.

(b) 3 Bf4

is sometimes called the London System--after the 1922 tournament in which it gained attention. The ideas behind the London System are much the same as the Colle, but with the important difference that if Black plays ...d7-d5 now, White obtains a terrific diagonal for his Bishop at h2-b8.

But there is an important difference between the London System after **1...g6, 2...Bg7** and the same opening against **1...Nf6, 2...g6**. In the former move order, Black controls the **e5** square immediately. This allows him to kick back at the Bishop: **3 Bf4, d6 4 e3, Nd7!** and **5...e5**, e.g. **5 h3, e5 6 Bh2, Qe7 7 Be2, Ngf6 8 0-0, 0-0 9 c4, Ne4! 10 dxe5, dxe5 11 Nfd2, Nxd2 12 Nxd2, f5 13 Qb3, a5 14 Rfd1, a4** and Black held a slight edge in **(Dzhindzikashvili-Soltis, Heraldica, New York 1979)**. Also see Illustrative Game at end of Variation A.

Also **5 c4, e5 6 Bg3, Nh6** and **...f7-f5**, burying the Bishop, or **6 dxe5, dxe5 7 Bg5, f6 8 Bh4, Nh6!** e.g. **9 Nc3, Nf5 10 Bg3, c6 11 e4, Nxg3 12 hxg3, Qe7 13 Be2, Nc5 14 Qd2, a5 15 b3, Be6** with advantage-- **Terebesi-Hardicsay, Hungary 1978.**

(c) 3 Nbd2

is among several quiet moves (*3 c3, 3 Nc3*) which fail to threaten Black's composure. Now that **Bf4** has been delayed, Black should feel comfortable answering the Knight moves with **3...d5!** Then **4 e3** would be passive and very similar to (a), while **4 g3, Nf6 5 Bg2** lacks enough influence on the center to hope for advantage, e.g. **5...0-0 6 0-0, c6 7 c4, Bf5 8 b3, Ne4 9 Bb2, Qa5 10 a3, Nd7 11 b4, Qd8 12 Rc1, b5** (**Tseshkovsky-Dvoretsky, U.S.S.R. Championship 1974**).

(d) There is greater point to the waiting-move **3 c3,**

since **3...d5 4 Bf4** gets White into his London System with a clean diagonal for the Bishop. There is nothing particularly wrong with that. But more in keeping with Black's "Indian" strategy is **3...Nf6** and, if **4 Bf4**, then **4...d6 5 e3, Nh5 6 Bg5, h6 7 Bh4, g5**. If White wants to preserve his Bishop with **5 h3**, then **5...0-0 6 e3, Nc6!** prepares Black for the Bishop-restricting push of the e-pawn e.g. **7 d5?, e5!; or 7 Bd3, Nh5 8 Bh2, e5** or **7 Bb5, a6 8 Ba4, b5 9 Bc2, Nd7** and **10...e5** or **9 Bb3, Na5 10 Bc2, Nc4 (Bisquier-Gligoric, Stockholm 1962)**.

Back to the main line after **3 Bg5:**

3...   Nf6

    The game now turns toward a somewhat rare version of the King's Indian Defense. White's Bishop may turn out to be a useful pinning piece on the **h4-d8** diagonal, or it may end up being kicked around by Black pawns.

4 Nbd2   d5!?

This cuts down White's options a bit, compared with **4...d6 5 e4** or **5 e3**. Once White's Queen Knight is developed at **d2**, he can't get much of an initiative by attacking **d5** with **c2-c4**.

5 e3	0-0
6 c3	Nbd7

The Knight goes to this square because Black may want to keep the **c6** clear in case he fianchettoes his Queen Bishop, and also because he may want to support **...c7-c5**. That support was not essential earlier since **6 Bd3, c5 7 dxc5** could have been met by **7...Qa5**, but after **6 c3** White has **b2-b4** to connect his pawns.

On **6 Bd3, c5** White would likely continue **7 c3** after which **7...Qb6 8 Rb1, Nbd7** and **9...e5!** should equalize, e.g. **9 0-0, e5! 10 Nxe5, Nxe5 11 dxe5, Ng4 12 Nf3, Nxe5 13 Nxe5, Bxe5 14 f4, Bf6!** or **9 Qa4, e5! 10 Nxe5, Nxe5 11 dxe5, Ng4 12 Be7, Nxe5 (Malanyuk-Georgadze, Lvov 1986** which went *13 Be2, Bd7 14 Qa3, Rfc8* since *13 Bxf8, Nxd3ch 14 Ke2, Bxf8 15 Kxd3, Bf5ch* would have been even worse).

A common theme for White in this variation is an early **b2-b4** to stop **...c7-c5**, or to force an opening of Queenside lines. But in the above line, **6 Bd3, c5 7 c3, Qb6 8 Rb1, Nbd7** the idea of **9 b4, cxb4 10 cxb4** makes **10...e5!** even stronger than normal: **11 Nxe5, Nxe5 12 dxe5, Ng4** or **11 dxe5, Ng4 12 Nd4, Ngxe5 13 Be2, Nc6!** with the idea of **14 N2f3, Nf6** and **15...Ne4** or **14 Nxc6, bxc6 15 0-0, Nf6 16 Bd3, a5!** as in O. Rodriguez-Georgadze, Pontevedra 1986.

7 Be2

On **d3** the Bishop temporarily prevents Black from occupying **e4**. But Black will play for **...e7-e5** and the threat of a fork on **e4** is annoying, e.g. **7 Bd3, c6 8 0-0, Qe8** as in the main line below. On **8 e4**, of course, **8...dxe4 9 Nxe4, Nxe4 10 Bxe4** is a position from Section I, Variation A1 with Black having an extra tempo.

7...	c6

This appears to be the easiest method of equalizing, but the immediate **7...Qe8**, threatening **8...e5**, has its points (*7...Qe8 8 0-0, e5 9 dxe5, Nxe5 10 Bf4, Nxf3ch 11 Bxf3, Qe7* with equality according to Zapata).

To stop **8...e5** White can try **Ne5** or **8 Bf4**. On **8 Ne5, Nxe5 9 dxe5, Nd7** White's center is loosened (*10 f4, f6!; 10 Nf3, c6*). But on **8 Bf4** Black must take time to protect the c-pawn, and after **8...c6** Black's threat of **...Nh5** can be answered by **9 Ne5!** with a slight edge.

8 0-0	Qe8
9 Re1	

It's difficult to stop Black from pushing the e-pawn now. On **9 Bf4, Nh5 10 Bc7** we have **10...f5!**, which favors Black's Stonewall formation (*...Nf6-e4*). The point of **9 Re1** is to meet **9...e5 10 dxe5, Nxe5** with **11 Bf4, Nxf3ch 12 Bxf3** with a slight pull.

9...	h6!
10 Bh4	

Again **10 Bf4** is met by **10...Nh5 11 Bc7, f5!**

10...	Ne4

And Black, with **11...f5** coming up, has equal play. **Cifuentes-Zapata, Dieren 1987** went **11 Nxe4, dxe4 12 Nd2, f5 13 f3** (else *13...e5!* favors Black), **exf3 14 gxf3** and now **14...e5 15 f4!, g5** was OK for Black, but **14...g5** and **15...e5** would have been more exact.

Note that in this last line Black is better after **14 Nxf3, e5!** or **14 Bxf3, g5 15 Bg3, e5**.

ILLUSTRATIVE GAME
Mortazavi-Colin McNab
Hastings Challengers, 1986-87

1 d4	d6

This vague move is winning converts because it allows Black to meet **2 c4** with **2...e5!?**, an allegedly superior form of the Old Indian Defense, and **2 Nf3** with **2...Bg4**.

The drawback to **1...d6** from our point of view is that that **2 e4** leads to a Pirc or Modern Defense in which Black has denied himself the central-blocKing **...c7-c6** and **...d7-d5** that we analyzed earlier. But after **2 Nf3, g6** we transpose into a previous chapter.

2 Nf3	g6
3 Bf4	Bg7
4 e3	Nd7!

Correctly appreciating the difference between this order of moves and that of the King's Indian Defense (*4...Nf6?!*). Black now achieves a tempo-gaining punch in the center.

5 h3	e5
6 Bh2	Ne7

At one time, masters turned up their noses when they saw a player post his Knights on the second rank, in front of King and Queen. Now some regard it as the height of sophistication. Black prepares castling and eyes **f5** for his Knight.

7 Bc4?	0-0
8 0-0	d5!

Why not? If White is going to take so little interest in the pawn-action of the center, he deserves what happens to him. Notice that if Black's pawns were posted at **d5** and **e6**, or the White pawns at **e4** and **d3**, the position would be much less clear.

9 Bb3	e4
10 Nfd2	c5

Black enjoys a virtual free hand in the center and now concerns himself with fine lines for his Rooks. Either of his Bishop-pawns can be advanced and, in fact, he pushes both. True, White's Bishop at **h2** now has an excellent six-square line of fire. But watch what happens to this diagonal.

11 c3	**Kh8**
12 Bc2	**f5**
13 dxc5	

This clears away **d4** for a Knight, but this hardly makes up for five or six other lousy pieces. But if White doesn't do something quickly, he will be opened up by **...g6-g5** and **...f5-f4/...Nf5** without a shred of counterplay.

13...	**Nxc5**
14 Nb3	**Ne6**
15 Nd4	**g5**
16 f3	**Qb6!**

The Queen takes aim at the weakened **e3** square as well as **b2**.

17 Bb3	**f4**

That does it for that fine Bishop on **h2**. Now **18 exf4, Nxd4 19 cxd4** loses material, however Black captures on **d4**.

18 fxe4	**Nxd4**
19 cxd4	**dxe4**
20 Nc3	**Nf5**
21 Nd5	**Qd8**

Now the **e3/d4** battlefront cannot be held and Black will push the enemy back with **...Be6** and **...Ne3**.

22 exf4	**Be6**
23 Nc7?	

A poor move in a poor position, based on **23...Qxc7 24 Bxe6** when White's position is merely bad.

23...	**Bxb3!**

White resigns. He loses a full piece (*24 Qc1, Rc8*).

Variation B
White plays the English Opening

> 1 c4   g6
> 2 Nc3

Here **2 e4** is sometimes played, so as to avoid transposition to the Gruenfeld Defense (*2 d4, Nf6 3 Nc3, d5*). But since we have no interest in the Gruenfeld, we'd answer **2 e4** with **2...Bg7** and then **3...d6**.

> 2...   Bg7

The English can be compared to Section II in this way: Black attacks the **d4** square early on and often wins at least temporary control of it. However in the English, White's d-pawn is held back at **d2** or **d3**, whereas in the Section II positions it has been coaxed to **d5**.

3 g3

With **3 e3** (*3...d6 4 d4*) White slips into a version of Section II in which he keeps some control of **d4**. But this is somewhat passive and Black should hit back with **4...Nc6** and **5...e5**.

The fianchetto begun by **3 g3** is a natural English Opening procedure. More flexible is **3 Nf3**, which postpones for at least a move the disclosure of White's plans. Black has a good waiting move in **3...d6** and then

4 d4, Bg4 leads into Section II, note to **4 e4**. If instead White plays **4 d3**, then **4...Nc6** or **4...e5** should transpose into the main line below. And **4 g3, Nc6** should do the same.

3...	e5
4 Bg2	d6

Black makes no Knight commitments and thereby leaves himself the option of either **...c7-c6** or **...Nc6** and also of **...Nf6** or **Ne7**. He also stops **d2-d4** by White, an advance that makes the opening a King's Indian Defense--something perfectly sound, but out of our repertoire.

If White insists on pushing his d-pawn two squares with **5 e3** as preparation, then **5...f5 6 d4, Nf6** is perfectly sound. The **7 dxe5** endgame is as usual, equal, and the **7 Nge2, 0-0 8 b4** middlegame reveals White to have plenty of weak squares after **8...e4! 9 Qb3, Be6 10 0-0, Bf7 11 f3, d5 (Korchnoi-Timman, Match 1976)** when Black has the pleasant choice of putting a pawn or Knight on **c6**. In either case, Black has a nice game.

Note that the delay in the decision over **c6** also helps Black in variations such as **5 e3, f5 6 Nge2, Nf6 7 0-0, 0-0 8 d3, c6!** when Black has chances to push his d-pawn advantageously (*9 b3, Na6 10 Ba3, Nc7 11 Qd2, Re8 12 e4?, d5!* as in **Garcia/Palermo-Janosevic, Lone Pine 1978** or *9 b4, Be6 10 b5, d5 11 bxc6, Nxc6!* and *11 cxd5, Nxd5!*).

5 Nf3

Some English Opening players always like to meet **...f7-f5** with **e2-e4** and therefore should try **5 d3, f5 6 e4**. Black should delay and probably avoid **...fxe4**, which gives up considerable influence on the **e4** square as well as the option of **...f5-f4**. Instead, he would prefer **6...c6 7 Nge2, Nf6** which retains the option of retaking on **f5** with Bishop or g-pawn, e.g. **8 0-0, 0-0 9 exf5, gxf5!?** which appears better than **9...Bxf5 10 d4**.

As Mikhail Botvinnik used to say, *"Every Russian schoolboy knows you must capture with the g-pawn in such positions"*, and here **9...gxf5 10 Bg5, h6! 11 Bxf6, Qxf6** or **10 f4?!, Qb6ch 11 Kh1, Ng4** is fine for the second player.

Black can also play for his own advance in the center **...d6-d5**. For example, **8 h3** (instead of *8 0-0*), **0-0 9 Be3, Be6** would transpose into **Ljubojevic-Kasparov, Linares 1992**, which continued **10 Qd2?, fxe4! 11 Nxe4, Nxe4 12 Bxe4, d5!** with an edge for Black. See the Illustrative Game.

5...	f5
6 0-0	Nf6

Now **7 d4** can be met by **7...e4** when **8 Ne1, 0-0 9 f3**--the only way for White to break into the center--leads after **9...exf3** to a fairly even position, e.g. **10 Bxf3, Nc6 11 Nc2, Ne7 12 d5, Nd7 13 Nd4, Ne5** or **12 Qd3?, c6 13 Bf4, d5 14 Be5, Be6 15 c5, Qd7 16 b4, g5!** followed by **...Ng6** (**Stolyar-Suetin, Olomouc 1975**).

7 d3	0-0

By delaying the entrance of his Queen Knight, Black has taken some of the sting out of **b2-b4-b5**, the natural source of White's middlegame play. If he decides at this late date to play **8 e4**, Black may decide to exploit **d4** with **8...Nc6**, or go in for **8...f4!? 9 gxf4, exf4 10 Bxf4, Nxe4**.

8 Rb1	a5
9 a3	Nh5

Black begins his Kingside counter-action, which will include the advance of his f-pawn and **...Bg4/...Qd7**. Now that Black's long-diagonal is open, he can meet **10 b4?** with **10...e4!** when both Knights are hanging. If White prepares for **b2-b4** with **10 Nd2**, then **10...Nc6! 11 b4, axb4 12 axb4, Nd4 13 c5, f4** offers equal chances (**Fedorowicz-Kagan, Hastings 1977-8**).

10 Qc2	f4
11 b4	axb4
12 axb4	Bg4

Now **...Nc6** and **...Bxf3** followed by **...Nd4** is in the air, and the retreat of **13 Nd2** makes **13...Nc6** even stronger.

13 b5

Here **13...Nd7** shows the wisdom of Black's delay in bringing this Knight into play. It will land on **c5** where it watches key squares such as **b3**, **e4** and **a4**.

Following **13...Nd7 14 Bb2, Nc5** play might continue **15 Ra1, Rxa1 16 Rxa1, Qd7** and the loss of the a-file is offset by Black's threats against the Kingside squares, such as **f2**. For example, **17 Ng5, Bh6 18 Nge4, Nxe4 19 Nxe4, Qf7!** and Black has a growing intiative.

In **Isaksen-Kristiansen, Esbjerg 1977** he gained momentum after **20 Bc1, Nf6 21 Nc3, Bc8! 22 Ra8, g5 23 Nd5, Ng4** and won soon after **24 Nxf4?, gxf4 25 Rxc8, fxg3!** (*26 Bd5, gxf2ch 27 Kf1, Nxh2ch*).

ILLUSTRATIVE GAME
Ljobomir Ljubojevic-Garry Kasparov
Linares 1992

1 c4	g6
2 Nc3	Bg7
3 g3	e5
4 Bg2	d6
5 d3	f5
6 e4	Nf6

Black's strategy now involves attacking the **c4**-pawn so that the **d3**-pawn is overloaded with responsibility: it cannot defend both **e4** and **c4**.

7 Nge2	0-0
8 h3	c6
9 Be3	Be6!

This should force White's hand by the minor threat of **10...fxe4** - which White ignores. After **10 exf5, gxf5!** White has no more than equality (*11 f4*).

10 Qd2?	fxe4!
11 Nxe4	Nxe4
12 Bxe4	d5

13 cxd5	cxd5
14 Bg2	Nc6
15 0-0	Qd7

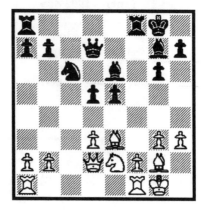

Black, with the superior center, greater space and more fluid development, already has a slight advantage. Kasparov now makes the kind of decision that distinguishes great players from the merely good. He concedes White's control of **e4** in order to gain the use of **d5**.

16 Kh2	d4!
17 Bg5	Bd5
18 Be4	Rf7
19 Kg2	Qe6!

The winner pointed out his threat is not only to win the a-pawn but to play **20...Bxe4 21 dxe4, h6!** and if **22 Bxh6, Bxh6 23 Qxh6**, then **23...Rh7!** wins on the h-file.

| 20 Bxd5 | Qxd5ch |
| 21 f3 | a5 |

This signals a switch to the Queenside, while White overprotects **h3**. Black will shoot the a-pawn to the sixth rank to create a hole at **c3**.

22 h4	a4
23 Ng1	a3
24 Rfb1	Bf8!

25 bxa3	Rxa3
26 Rb2	b5

Black's game is strategically won: He can bombard the pawns at **a2** and **d3** with Rooks and a Knight (*...Na5-b7-c5*) while White is bereft of counterplay.

27 Rfb1	b4
28 Rc2	Rc3
29 Rbb2	Na5!

In the *Informant*, Kasparov gave a sample winning line: **30 Qe2, Rfc7 31 Nh3, h6 32 Bc1, Qc5! 33 Rxc3, Qxc3** and wins.

30 Qd1	Nb7
31 Bd2!?	Rxd3
32 Qe2	Rdxf3!
33 Nxf3	d3

Black concludes matters nicely and White could have resigned within a few moves. The game represents testimony to what happens when White loses the battle for **d5** without a fight.

34 Qe3	dxc2
35 Rxc2	Nc5
36 Bxb4	Nd3
37 Bd2	

Or **37 Bxf8, Rxf3** and Black wins just as easily (*38 Qxf3, Ne1ch*).

37...	Bc5
38 Rxc5?!	Nxc5
39 Bc3	Nd3
40 a4	Rc7
41 Bd2	Nb2!

And White resigned after **42 Bc3, Nc4 43 Qe2, Rf7 44 a5, e4 45 Ne1, e3ch 46 Kg1, Nd2.**

Variation C
White plays a Reti-like System

1 Nf3   g6

There is little independent value to **1 Nf3** if White plays **d2-d4** or **c2-c4** early on. For instance **2 c4, Bg7 3 Nc3, d6 4 d4, Bg4** is a position from Section II and **4 d3, e5** should reach one from Section III, Variation B. Perhaps **4 g3** is the trickiest since **4...e5** allows White to avoid transposition (*5 Bg2, f5*) with **5 d4**. Then Black can go into a King's Indian Defense with **5...Nf6** or, if he has a more enterprising attitude, adopt one of the less-traveled policies such as **5...e5** and **6...Nc6**.

We should also note **1 g3** may or may not transpose into our main line below, after **1...g6 2 Bg2, e5**. If White does not play **3 d4**, Black will end up either in Variation B (say with *3 c4*) or the main line below (with *3 Nf3*, for example). On **3 d4, exd4 4 Qxd4** Black plays **4...Nf6** and **5...Nc6** or **5...Bg7** with a useful gain of time, e.g. **4...Nf6 5 c4, Nc6 6 Qd3, Bg7 7 Nc3, d6 8 Nf3, 0-0 9 0-0, Nd7** and **10...Nc5** possibly followed by **...f7-f5**.

2 g3

There is no point to **2 b3?!** if White has to meet **2...Bg7** with **3 c3, 3 Nc3** or **3 d4**. Also, with **2 c3, Bg7 3 d4** we reach note (c) to Variation A of this section.

2...	Bg7
3 Bg2	e5

This advance fits in well in some lines in which White's Knight appears prematurely developed on **f3** and he cannot hit back in the center with **e2-e3/Nge2/d2-d4** or **f2-f4**.

Now **4 c4, f5** or **4 0-0, f5** should reach positions from Variation B. Relatively unexplored is **4 d4**, but **4...e4** and **5...f5** seems to equalize fairly easily.

4 e4!?

With this, White hopes to obtain a favorable King's Indian Reversed position, with **d2-d3, Nbd2, Nh4** and **f2-f4**. He also may be thinking of **5 d4**, now that **5...e4** is not a playable response.

4...	c5

Playing into a Sicilian Defense stops White from advancing in the center. The fact that White's King Knight is developed on **f3** means that the only way he can change the pawn structure in the center is with **f2-f4**, after moving the Knight.

5 0-0	Nc6
6 d3	

White doesn't have enough firepower to make **d2-d4** work: **6 c3, Nge7 7 Na3, 0-0 8 Nc2** could be met by **8...d5** with a nice game in the center for Black (*9 exd5, Nxd5 10 d4?!, exd4 11 cxd4, c4*). Black can also wait for White to do the pawn-pushing, e.g. **8...d6** and if **9 d4**, then **9...exd4 10 cxd4, Bg4.**

6...	Nge7

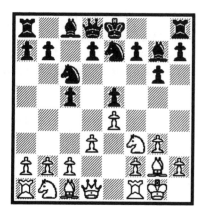

7 Nbd2

Now that the **d5** square is a major hole, White can consider **7 Nc3** when we have an orthodox Closed Variation of the Sicilian in which White's other Knight is misplaced because it blocks the **f2-f4-5** advance. If White tries to attack the enemy King with **7 Nc3, d6 8 Be3, 0-0 9 Qd2** and **Bh6**, Black equalizes quickly with **9...Nd4!** And the f-pawn advance with **8 Nh4, 0-0 9 f4** can be handled by **9...exf4 10 gxf4, f5** followed by ...**Be6, Qd7** and ...**Rae8**.

A more positional-minded plan is the occupation of the **d5** hole with **7 Nc3, d6 8 Nd2!?, 0-0 9 Nc4, Be6 10 Ne3**. Then Black must choose between expanding on the Queenside with ...**b7-b5-b4** and on the Kingside with ...**f7-f5-f4**. For example, **10...Rb8 11 a4, a6 12 Ncd5, b5 13 axb5, axb5** followed by **14...b4** and ...**Nd4** is double-edged. More ambitious is **10...f5** when **11...f4** is a nasty idea. Then **11 f4, exf4 12 gxf4, Qd7** is balanced and **11 exf5, gxf5 12 f4, d5!** is getting Black an upper hand.

The advance of the f-pawn comes upon White quickly in these lines. In **Biyiasas-Dzhdindzhikashvili, Lone Pine 1980**, White tried (by transposition) **7 c3, d6 8 Be3, 0-0** and decided that his bid for an open center was difficult to achieve since **9 d4** allows **9...exd4! 10 cxd4, Bg4** with strong pressure on **d4**. Instead, he shifted gears with **9 Nfd2, Be6 10 c4?** and found himself on the defensive following **10...f5 11 f3, Qd7 12 Nc3, f4! 13 Bf2, h5 14 Nd5, g5 15 Nb1, Ng6 16 Nbc3, Rf7**.

True, White had iron control of **d5**. But he had little to say about the dozen or so significant Kingside squares: **17 Kh1, Raf8 18 Ne2, g4! 19 Ng1, fxg3 20 hxg3, h4 21 Kh2, Nd4 22 Bxd4, hxg3ch 23 Kxg3, Qd8! 24 Kf2, exd4** and White resigned after **25 Ke1, Bxd5! 26 cxd5, Qh4ch 27 Kd2, Nf4.**

Black has an alternative policy involving **...d7-d5** himself. He should play **7...0-0** (rather than *7...d6*) in order to save a tempo. Then **8 Nh4** - a perfectly good strategy if Black intends **8...f5** - is met nicely by **8...d5!**. For example, **9 Nd2, Be6 10 f4, Qd7** with the kind of position that is considered slightly favorable in reversed form (in a normal King's Indian Defense), e.g. *11 Ndf3, exf4 12 gxf4, Rad8 13 Qe1, Bh3* - **Loginov-Ernst, Manila 1992**).

7...	d6
8 a4	0-0

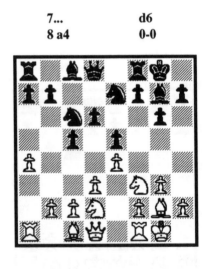

9 Nc4

Black can prepare now with **9...h6** followed by **...Qd7**. Or he can play **9...f5** directly, not fearing the opening of the **b3-g8** diagonal. If allowed, he will push to **f4** (*9...f5 10 Nh4, f4!*). If White exchanges on **f5**, then Black suddenly has four pawns in the center.

To counter this, White may prefer **9 Nh4** (instead of *9 Nc4*) and then **9...f5 10 f4** when **10...exf4 11 gxf4, Be6**, with thoughts of **12...d5**, is a typical complex position of modern chess. Black has ample counterplay.

Variation D
White Fianchettoes His Queen Bishop

The Queenside fianchetto with **1 b3**, and its lesser-known cousin, **1 b4**, gained some notoriety in the early 1970s and then faded out of fashion---for no particular reason. It poses a problem for us because it is the only way of absolutely stopping **2...Bg7**. (*1 b3, g6 2 Bb2, Bg7?? 3 Bxg7*). This is one reason never to start a correspondence game with the "if-moves" **1...g6** and **2...Bg7!**

1 b3

We'll consider **1 b4** positions in the same main line. Differences will be noted below.

1...	g6
2 Bb2	Nf6

A superficial look at **3 Bxf6, exf6** indicates White is doing well. But White has weakened himself on the long diagonal and after **...Bg7** and **...f6-f5**, he may have problems in the vicinity of c3 and d4. The extra f-pawn helps Black dominate the e-file. For example, **4 d4, f5 5 Nf3, Bg7 6 e3, 0-0 7 c4, d6 8 Nc3, Nd7 9 Be2, Nf6 10 0-0, Re8** and **...Ne4**.

A stunning alternative is **3 g4!?**, based on the long-diagonal pin and the idea of **3...Bg7 4 g5, Nh5 5 Bxg7, Nxg7 6 Qc1!** and **7 Qb2** with play along the weakened **b2-b7** line. But **3...h6!** stops the g-pawn in its tracks: **4 h4, Bg7 5 Bg2, d6 6 g5, hxg5 7 hxg5, Rxh1 8 Bxh1, Nh5 9 Bxg7, Nxg7 10 c4, e5** and Black has better chances of exploiting the Kingside than White.

3 Nf3

Besides this and the forceful **3 Bxf6** and **3 g4**, there are abundant choices after **1 b3, g6 2 Bb2, Nf6:**

(a) **3 e4** also takes advantage of the long-diagonal pin (*3...Nxe4?? 4 Bxh8*) and leads to **3...d6 4 g3, Bg7 5 Bg2, e5** positions that are similar to our main line except that White has his e-pawn, rather than c- or d-pawn on the fourth rank. That e-pawn can become a problem after **6 Ne2, 0-0 7 d4, exd4! 8 Nxd4, Re8** or **6 d4, exd4 7 Bxd4, Nc6 8 Bb2, 0-0**. Better is the quiet **6 Ne2, 0-0 7 0-0** after which **7...Re8** stops **8 d4** and **8 f4** (*8 f4, exf4 9 Nxf4, Nxe4* or *9 Rxf4, Nh5 10 Bxg7, Nxf4*).

White is left then with passive options in the center, such as **8 c4, Nc6 9 Nbc3, Nd7!** and **...Nc5-e6-d4**, or **8 Re1, c5!? 9 a4, Nc6 10 Na3, Be6 11 Nc4?, Nxe4! 12 f4, Bg4 13 Bxe4, d5** with advantage--**Bellon-Polu-gayevsky, Palma de Mallorca 1972**.

(b) **3 c4** should transpose into the main line below once White advances his d-pawn twice. If he does not, Black is sure to have a free hand in the center, e.g. **3...Bg7 4 Nc3, 0-0 5 g3** (*5 e4?, Nxe4*) **d5!** or **4 g3, 0-0 5 Bg2, d6 6 f4?!, Nc6 7 Nf3, e5 8 fxe5, Ng4.**

(c) **3 f4** is a Bird's Opening in which White has gotten the fianchetto that he doesn't achieve in the **1 f4, g6** move order.

Reasonable is the variation **4 Nf3** and **5 e3**, after **1 b3, g6 2 Bb2, Nf6 3 f4, Bg7 4 Nf3, 0-0 5 e3, d6** (*5...d6* prepares for the *...e5!?* punch that can be justified tactically). For example:

6 d4, Nbd7 7 c4, e5! 8 dxe5, dxe5 9 Nxe5, Ng4! 10 Nxd7, Bxb2 or **8 fxe5, dxe5 9 d5, Re8 10 Nc3, Ng4 11 Qd2, e4 12 h3?, Nxe3!--Linder-Bondarenko, U.S.S.R. 1960.**

White does better to keep lines modestly closed with **6 c4, e5 7 g3!?** when complex, balanced play arises after **7...exf4 8 gxf4, d5.**

Or he can play **6 Na3** with the idea of meeting **6...e5 7 fxe5, Ng4** with **8 Nc4!** (*8...Nxe5 9 Ncxe5. dxe5 10 Bxe5!, Bxe5 11 Nxe5, Qh4ch 12 g3* and White is clearly better). If White has played **1 b4** rather than **1 b3**, then in the last variation Black can partially justify his play with **12...Qxb4.** But even then **13 Bg2** and White holds the superior control of lines.

Therefore, Black may do better at move six to build up quietly with **6...b6.** For instance, with White's pawn on **b4**, the sequence **6 Na6, b6 7 Be2, c5!** turns out well for Black if the b-file is opened: **8 bxc5, bxc5 9 0-0, Nc6 10 Qe1?!, Rb8! 11 Rb1, Be6 12 Nc4, Rb4** with a slight edge, e.g. **13 Bxf6, Bxf6 14 Rxb4, Nxb4 15 c3, Nc6 16 h4, Na5.**

Back to the main line after **1 b3, g6 2 Bb2, Nf6 3 Nf3.**

| 3... | | Bg7 |

4 g3

On **4 e3, 0-0 5 Be2** White adopts a subtle setup sometimes favored by Nimzovich. Since **5...d6** (then *6...e5!*) threatens to deny White any serious chance for central advantage, White should play **6 d4** after which **6...Nbd7 7 0-0, e5!** leads to play as in our main line (*8 dxe5, Ng4*) but without White's domination of the **g2-b7** diagonal. On **8 c4, Re8 9 Qc2, c6**

10 Nc3, Qe7 11 Rfd1, e4! 12 Nfd2, Nf8 we have typical play of certain King's Indian Defense and King's Indian Reversed positions, with Black having a Kingside attack brewing with **...h7-h5** and **...Nf8-h7-g5.**

In these positions White's play comes from the advance of his Queenside pawns, and for that reason **1 b4** may be better than **1 b3.** After **1 b4, g6**

2 Bb2, Nf6 3 Nf3, Bg7 4 e3, 0-0 5 c4, d6 6 d4, Black can continue **6...Nbd7** and **7...e5**, or delay a decision about his Queen Knight in favor of **6...e6, 7...Qe7 and 8...e5.** For example, **6...e6 7 Nc3, Qe7 8 Be2, e5 9 0-0, e4! 10 Nd2, Re8 11 b5, h5**

and both sides have staked out their terrain--White on the Queenside, Black on the Kingside. Each player wants open lines, but Black will be less interested in files for his Rooks than in shifting minor pieces and his Queen to his left.

Typical play would then be **12 a4, Bf5 13 a5, Nbd7 14 a6! b6! 15 Rc1, Rac8 16 Ba3, Nf8 17 Na2, Ne6 18 Nb4**. White has won control of **c6** and he will advance his c-pawn, thereby assuring at least one open file. However, the King's are on the other side of the board and Black is not worse after **18...Qd7 19 Qb3, Ng5 20 Nc6, Bg4 21 f3, exf3 22 Nxf3, Bh6 23 Rc3, Nge4 24 Rc2, Bf5 25 Bc1, Ra8 26 Bd3, g5!--Sander-Korchnoi, Biel 1985**.

A somewhat slower system for White is revealed in this move order: **1 b4, g6 2 Bb2, Nf6 3 Nf3, Bg7 4 e3, d6 5 d4, 0-0 6 Nbd2!?, Nbd7 7 c4, e5 8 Nb3, Re8 9 Be2**.

The idea is recapture on **d4** with a piece, but **9...e4 10 Nd2, Nf8 11 Qc2, Bf5** is good for Black---**12 h3, h5 13 a4, Qd7 14 a5, b6** or **14 Nb1, c6 15 Nc3, b6 16 Ba3, Ne6 17 b5, c5 18 0-0-0, cxd4 (Chepukaitis-Yermolinsky, U.S.S.R. 1980)**.

Back to the main line after **4 g3** (*1 b3, g6 2 Bb2, Nf6 3 Nf3, Bg7 4 g3*)

4...	**0-0**
5 Bg2	

If White inserts **c2-c4** around here, he actually restricts his chances. See the note to White's seventh move below.

5...   **d6**
6 d4

This is necessary at some point, or Black's **...e7-e5** will leave him unchallenged in the center. The bad point about White's **1 b3** is that it slows up some of the Queenside strategies that work well against **...e7-e5**, but which require a quick **Rb1** and **b2-b4-b5**.

6...   **Nbd7**

This looks to be the most accurate. On **6...Nfd7** for example, Black gets a fine game from **7 Nc3!, e5 8 Qd2!** followed by Queenside castling (*8...Re8 9 dxe5, Nxe5 10 Nxe5, Bxe5 11 0-0-0*--**Olafsson-Kavalek, Wijk aan Zee 1969**). Then his delay in moving his c-pawn works out well.

More significantly, White's move order also allows him to meet **6...e5** with **7 dxe5, Ng4 8 h3!**, leading to an exchange of pieces that is favorable when White has avoided moving his c-pawn, e.g. **8...Nxe5 9 Nxe5, dxe5 10 Qxd8, Rxd8 11 Nd2** and **12 0-0-0** or **9...Bxe5 10 Nc3!, c6 11 Qd2** with Queenside castling (*11...d5 12 0-0-0, Qe7 13 h4!, a5 14 f4, Bg7 15 h5-*--**Keene-Pares, Torremolinos 1975**).

Before leaving the subject, we should mention that in different orders, Black can have an easier time. Suppose White delays **Bb2?** This occurs in, say, **1 d4 Nf6 2 Nf3, g6 3 g3, Bg7 4 Bg2, d6 5 0-0, 0-0 6 b3**--then **6...Nbd7** and **7...e5** will transpose into the above positions.

But more accurate is **6...e5!** which punishes White's sloppy order (*7 Bb2, e4! or 7 dxe5, Ng4*). Black can even meet **7 dxe5** with **7...dxe5** and **8...e4** because **8 Nxe5** is met by **8...Ng4**. If after **7...dxe5** White tries **8 Ba3**, Black can play **8...Qxd1 9 Rxd1, Re8** and then **10 Nc3, e4** and **11...e3**, whereas **8 Bb2** allows **8...e4** with a fine game (*9 Qxd8, Rxd8 10 Ng5, Bf5 11 Na3, h6 12 Rad1, Nbd7 13 Nh3, c6 14 Nc4, Nd5* as in **Dreyer-Gligoric, Dublin 1957**).

7 0-0

Here **7 c4** has been played. Or it could have been played earlier--at any point from move three on--and the result whould have been the same. The pawn move is not that useful here, since the c4 square may be needed for a Knight later on. After **7 c4, e5 8 dxe5, Ng4 9 0-0, dxe5** Black is preparing a push of the e-pawn (*10 Nbd2, e4! 11 Nxe4, Bxb2; or 11 Bxg7, exf3 12 exf3, Nxh2*). Gufeld says **10 Nfd2** would favor White, but this is unclear: **10...c6 11 h3, Nh6 12 c5!?, Nd7 13 b4, f5 14 Nc4, Nf7.**

Instead of simplifying in the center, White can play **8 e3** with the idea of **8...exd4 9 Bxd4!**, taking advantage of Black's inability now to play ...Nc6. But Black stands fairly well after **8...Re8 9 0-0, e4**, e.g. **10 Nfd2, Nf8 11 Nc3, Bf5 12 f3, exf3 13 Qxf3, c6 14 e4, Bg4** (**Nikolaevsky-Kasparov, U.S.S.R. 1978**).

7...   Re8

Extra safe. With **7...e5 8 dxe5, Ng4 9 h3**, Black may face some slight problems. For an example of **7...e5**, see Illustrative Game at end of Variation D.

8 Nbd2

This eyes **c4** for a Knight. With **8 c4**, we transpose into the note to White's seventh move.

8...   e5
9 dxe5

With **9 e4** White stops the e-pawn from gathering space. But then **9...exd4 10 Nxd4, Nc5** is a better position for Black than he usually gets from the King's Indian Defense (*11 f3, d5; or 11 Re1, Bg4 12 f3, Bd7*).

9...	dxe5
10 e4	b6

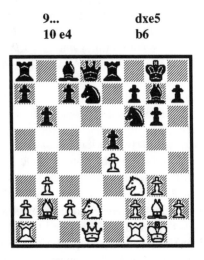

The White e-pawn is as much of a target as Black's after this. The mutual exchange of pawns--**11 Nc4, Bb7 12 Ncxe5, Nxe5 13 Nxe5, Bxe4**-- is fine for Black. Better is **11 Re1** when **11...Bb7 12 a4, a5** is balanced. **Pomar-Browne, Orense 1977** shows how quickly Black can get the upper hand: **13 h3, Qc8 14 Qc1?, Bh6! 15 Qb1** (or *15 Qd1, Rd8!*)**, Nc5 16 Qa2, Ncxe4.**

ILLUSTRATIVE GAME
W. Hartston-M. Najdorf
Hastings 1971-72

| 1 Nf3 | Nf6 |

If you want to stay in one of the systems recommended earlier in these pages, Black's second move is not for you. True, it stops **2 e4** and would transpose into King's Indian Defense positions after **2 d4, g6**, or the like after **2 b3, 2 b4**, et cetera. But **2 c4** would likely lead to positions we've not considered. This game illustrates our recommendations for Black against the double fianchetto.

2 g3

There are very few true Hypermodernists left in the chess world-- people who believe in **1 Nf3** with semi-religious fervor. There are however, quite a few people who have sensibly adopted the Knight move as a backup system for opening a game when they are uncertain about their usual **1 e4** or **1 d4**.

2...	g6
3 b3	Bg7
4 Bb2	0-0
5 Bg2	d6
6 d4	

Note White's avoidance of **c2-c4**, the hallmark of most King's Indian-like positions. Since White's Queen has no direct access to the Queenside because **b3** is occupied, and since neither player has professed intentions of occupying **d5** with a pawn, the **c2-c4** advance is often dispensed with. It can always be inserted later, as White does in this game.

| 6... | Nbd7 |

Two days before this game was played, Miguel Najdorf held the White pieces (vs. V. Ciocaltea) and obtained a small edge after **6...e5 7 dxe5, Ng4 8 Nbd2, Nc6 9 0-0, Re8 10 Rb1** because Black recaptured on e5 with a Knight: **10...Ngxe5?! 11 Nxe5, dxe5 12 e3, Bf5 13 Ne4, Qxd1 14**

Rbxd1. Black's cramped position seems to work best, ironically, with an extra pair of Knights on the board, as in this game.

	7 0-0	**e5**

Black plays this thrust instead of our covered **7...Re8**.

The alternative of breaking in the center, **...c7-c5**, fits in badly here, particularly with Black's Knight on **d7**. White could meet **7...c5** with **8 c4, cxd4 9 Nxd4** and build a Maroczy Bind center (*e2-e4!*). Or he could push his d-pawn at some point to the fifth rank, after which Black's natural **...e7-e6** break is hard to achieve and his Knight sits inconveniently on **d7**, now that **...Na6-c7** is denied.

	8 dxe5	**Ng4**
	9 c4	**Re8**

There's no rush to recapture on **e5** as long as the White pawn is pinned. Black wants to make sure he can retake with a pawn, establishing the more mobile center.

	10 h3	**Nh6**
	11 Qc2	**dxe5**

Time to evaluate: the middlegame starts here. There is one open file and White will surely be the first to occupy it. Because Black cannot allow an enemy Knight unrestricted access to **d5** (or even *b5*) we can expect **...c7-c6**. That grants White a hole at **d6**. White will complete his development shortly, but it is not at all clear where Black's Queen Bishop will end up.

Sound one-sided so far? There's more to it. White can occupy that one square, **d6**, but he can do it only with difficulty (after *...Qe7* and *...Nf7*) and then only with a Rook or Bishop--not the piece that would really hurt, a Knight. And the occupation of **d6** is the only natural plan for White.

He does not have a quick method of favorably opening up the Queenside and there is little to be gained in the center. He can stabilize matters there with **12 e4**, but after **12...f6** followed by **...Qe7, ...Nf7** and perhaps **...Re8, ...Nf8** and ...Bishop-somewhere, Black should stand well.

Moreover, we can't ignore the presence in the center of one crucial middlegame player, the Black e-pawn. If he is joined by his brother f-pawn on the fourth rank, and advances to the fifth, then White will have lost a major share of the center. He may have access to **d4** and, after the inevitable exchange of the dark-squared Bishops, he will have the theoretical advantage of "the better Bishop" in the remaining stage of play. But Black will have the space.

12 Rd1?!	**f5!**
13 Nbd2	**e4!**

The player who believes in **1...g6** will often have to part with his Bishop in this kind of exchange. It generally leaves his Kingside a bit weaker. But it also leaves White's Queenside more vulnerable, i.e. **c3, a3, b4**. And Black will cover many of the key squares with **...Qf6**. Here the exchange and central advance give Black an early edge.

14 Bxg7	**Kxg7**
15 Nd4	**c6**

This last move by Black was inevitable (*15...Qf6 16 Nb5*). White has an excellent Knight outpost at **d4**, but it will be easily balanced by the Black Knight that will reach **e5**. Thanks to the pawn structure, Black can expand on the Kingside with **...h5-h4**, or **...Nf7-g5**, or even a well-timed **...f5-f4**. White cannot compete on even terms on that wing and must try to exploit Black's last move with **b3-b4-b5**, coupled perhaps with **c4-c5**. The immediate **16 b4** is called for.

16 Nf1?	**Qf6**
17 b4	**Ne5**
18 Rab1	**Nhf7**

Now **19 c5** would be a preparatory move for **20 b5**, but after **19...Be6**, Black will have solved his only remaining middlegame problem--- his Bishop.

19 Nd2	**a5**

It's always appealing to challenge moves like **17 b4** with a later **...a7-a5** when it means opening the a-file that your opponent's Queen Rook has abandoned. This is effective here, since White is not ready for **20 b5** because of **20...c5!** and **21...b6**, closing down the Queenside.

20 a3	**axb4**
21 axb4	**h5!**

Black's plan is simple: He will weaken g3 and h2 with **...h5-h4xg3**, followed by **...Ng5**. Even with a Knight at f1 and his Bishop at g2, White's King position is difficult to defend, and **22 h4, e3 23 fxe3, Ng4** would be awful. His next move indicates the extent of his concern about his King.

22 f4	**exf3 e.p.**
23 exf3	**Ng4!**

The threats are **24...Qxd4ch** and **24...Ne3**. After the coming exchange, Black will be threatening to overwhelm the Kingside by pushing his f-pawn. (But not the immediate *23...f4?* because of *24 Ne4!*).

24 Nf1	**Ne3**
25 Nxe3	**Rxe3**
26 Qd2	**f4!**

Now was the time. One Bishop is buried, the other given life. Najdorf points out the terrible trap lying in **26...Qg5?** which walks into **27 f4!**, **Qxg3 28 Ne2!**, when White wins.

27 gxf4	**Raa3**

And not **27...Qxf4? 28 Nc2**. Note how the Black Rooks now dominate.

28 Nc2	**Rad3**
29 Nxe3	

Desperation comes early this year. On **29 Qf2** Black exploits the weakened Queenside with **29...Rxd1ch** and **30...Rc3 31 c5, Qxf4 32 Qd4ch, Qxd4 33 Nxd4, Rc4**.

29...	Rxd2
30 Rxd2	Qxf4
31 Rb3	Ng5

Ordinarily, two Rooks are superior to the Queen, but Black's superior Kingside play is not ordinary. The h-pawn is lost and with it the rest of the King protection.

32 Rbd3	Bxh3
33 Nf1	Qxc4
34 Rd4	Nxf3ch!

A little finishing touch.

| 35 Bxf3 | Qxf1ch |
| 36 Kh2 | Qxf3 |

White resigns.

There's not much left after **37 R(4)d3, Qf1** since **38 Rxh3** loses a Rook to **38...Qf4ch**.

Variation E
White Plays Bird's Opening

1 f4   g6

The favorite opening move of Henry Bird, **1 f4**, evades the central controversies of Sections I and II. It allows Black to play **...c7-c5** or **...d7-d5**--or both if he wishes.

2 Nf3

It's already too late to smoothly fianchetto the Queen Bishop (*2 b3, Bg7!*). Alternative schemes of development, begun by **2 g3** or **2 e3**, will transpose into one of the notes to move three below. The most distinct road to independent positions is **2 g3, Bg7 3 Bg2** and **4 Nh3!?** followed by Nf2-- the so-called Paris Attack. A good antidote is a rapid advance of Black's two center pawns, e.g. **3...d5 4 Nh3, Nf6 5 Nf2, Nbd7 6 0-0, e5** or **6 d4, c5** and **...b7-b6.**

2...   Bg7

3 e3

This flexible system, leaving the option of a one- or two-square advance of the d-pawn, works better for White when Black has played some other way with his first two moves. If Black has played, say, **1 f4, c5 2 Nf3, d5 3 e3, Nc6?!** White could find an excellent square for his King Bishop on **b5**. Or, if Black had played an early **...e7-e6**, then White might post that Bishop effectively at **d3**, e.g. **1 f4, Nf6 2 Nf3, e6 3 e3, b6 4 Bd3!?**

White also has these options:

(a) 3 e4 suddenly turns us back into the King-Pawn territory of Section I. After **3...d5 4 e5, h5** Black begins his now familiar strategy of occupying the light-colored squares (*...Bg4/...Nh6-f5*, etc.).

(b) 3 c4 is a hybrid of English and Bird, a strange but not particularly ugly animal. Black can then play to push his d- or e-pawn, or both. One method of developing smoothly is **3...Nf6 4 e3, 0-0 5 Nc3, d5** followed, if permitted, by **...c7-c5** and perhaps **...d5-d4**.

After **6 b3, c5! 7 d4** (else the d-pawn advances) White is just too loosely hung together: **7...Ne4! 8 Bb2, Qa5 9 Rc1, Bg4! 10 Be2, cxd4 11 Nxd4, Bxe2 12 Qxe2, Nc6 13 cxd5, Nxd4 14 exd4, Nxc3 15 Bxc3, Qxd5** and Black has a clear advantage (**Seidman-Reshevsky, New York 1939**).

If White is going to play **d2-d4**, he might as well do it at move six: **6 d4, c5 7 dxc5, Qa5 8 cxd5, Nxd5 9 Qxd5, Bxc3ch 10 Bd2, Bxd2ch 11**

Qxd2, Qxc5 with a position reminiscent of the Gruenfeld--but with **f2-f4** oddly inserted. In **Pirc-Alatortsev, Moscow 1935** Black missed several chances and only drew following **12 Rc1, Qb6 13 Bc4, Be6! 14 Bxe6, Qxe6 15 0-0, Nc6 16 a3, Rad8 17 Qc3, Rd7**. He may also do better at move eight with **8...Rd8**, intending **9...Ne4**.

(c) **3 g3** is the Bird Indian, a reversed form of the Dutch Indian. Our recommended antidote to this is **3...d5** followed by **4...Nd7** and a quick advance of the e-pawn.

For example **3...d5 4 Bg2, Nd7** and now **5 0-0, e5 6 fxe5, Nxe5 7 Nxe5, Bxe5 8 d3, Ne7 9 c3, 0-0 10 Bh6, Bg7 11 Bxg7, Kxg7** leaves Black with a bit more of the center than White. In **Zwaig-Farago, Hastings 1976-77** White did nothing more than equalize with **12 Qa4, c6 13 Qd4ch, f6 14 Qf2, Qb6 15 e4, dxe4 16 Bxe4, Bf5 17 Re1, Bxe4 18 Rxe4, Nd5**. Black can play for more, early on, with **10...Re8**.

A more active plan for White is **8 c4** (rather than *8 d3*), but the liquidation of the Black center gives him good open lines: **8...dxc4 9 Na3, Ne7 10 Kh1, 0-0 11 Nxc4, Bg7 12 d3, c6** and now **13 Bg5, h6 14 Bf4, Nd5!** favored Black in **Levitina-Kushnir, Match 1977** (which ended with *15 Bd2, Bg4 16 Ne3, Nxe3 17 Bxe3, Qd7 18 Qd2, Rfe8 19 Rf2??, Rxe3! 20 Qxe3, Bd4 21 Qf4, g5!*) White resigns.

3...   d5

There are a number of reasonable pawn structures at Black's disposal, including **...d7-d6/...e7-e5** and **...c7-c5/...d7-d6**. This text has the merit of simplicity. Now **4 c4** will transpose into note (b) of White's third move.

4 Be2

Delaying further a decision about the d-pawn, and thereby denying himself the opportunity to play his Bishop to **d3**. In the mid-1980s Black, in the Dutch Defense, began to challenge the long standing contention that if Black adopts a Stonewall pawn structure with **...d7-d5, ...e7-e6** and **...f7-e5**, he should post his Bishop at **e7** rather than at **d6**. The reasoning against **...Bd6** is that White could then weaken the enemy's center with **Bf4!?**

After **4 d4**,

Nf6 5 Bd3, most attention has focused on **5...0-0 6 0-0, c5 7 c3, b6**, which prepares the exchange of Bishops with **...Ba6** and also protects Black's c-pawn. Routine attacking procedures for White can then give him a poor game positionally. For example, on **8 Bd2,** with the idea of reaching **h4** via **e1,** Black plays **9...Ba6** with a good game: **9 Bxa6, Nxa6 10 Qe2, Qc8 11 Be1, Nc7 12 Nbd2, Qb7 13 Ne5, Nce8!** and ...Nd6 seems fine for him (**Dreyer-van Scheltinga, Dublin 1957**).

If White stops the exchange of Bishops with **8 Qe2,** then **8...Bf5** appears indicated. The weakening of the King position from **9 Bxf5, gxf5** can be minimized if Black defends accurately, e.g. **10 Ne5, e6 11 Kh1, Nbd7 12 Nd2, Kh8 13 Rg1, Nxe5 14 fxe5, Ng4 15 Nf3, f6.**

Relatively unexplored are the positions arising after **8 Nbd2, Ba6 9 Bxa6, Nxa6 10 Ne5** when both sides reinforce the occupation square "e5"--White with **Nd2-f3** and Black with ...Nc7-e8-d6.

Back to **4 Be2:**

4...   **Nf6**

There are good arguments in favor of developing the Knight on **h6** or for playing **4...c5,** but the simple, direct **4...Nf6** is easiest to handle.

5 0-0   **0-0**

6 d3

There are two major alternatives here. One is **6 d4,** another form of the Stonewall. Black should proceed with a swap of light-squared Bishops as he did in the note to White's fourth move above: **6...c5 7 c3, b6 8 Qe1** (note that *8 Qe2* is not possible here), **e6 9 Nbd2, Ba6**. For example, **Briem -A. Arnason, Reykjavik, 1982** favored Black soon after **10 Ne5, Bxe2 11 Qxe2, Nfd7 12 b3, f6 13 Nxd7, Nxd7 14 c4, f5 15 Bb2, a5**.

The other idea here is **6 Ne5**, a reversed form of an idea of Alexander Alekhine's from the Dutch Defense. Before White can coordinate his minor pieces with **Bf3, Qe2** and **d2-d4**, Black can play **6...Nbd7 7 Bf3, Nxe5! 8 fxe5, Ne4** with adequate play: **9 d3, Ng5** or **9 c4, Bxe5 10 cxd5, Ng5 11 d4, Bg7 12 Nc3, Nxf3ch 13 Qxf3, Bd7--Gusev-Geller, U.S.S.R. 1970**.

6...	c5
7 Qe1	

This is the basic attacking plan of the Bird's and of it's Dutch Defense relative. White has a problem with his Queenside pieces since the natural **7 Nc3** allows **7...d4!**, gaining valuable space. The Knight can go to **d2**, but the immediate **7 Nbd2** is discouraged by **7...Ng4** when **e3** is hard to cover. Therefore, White prepares **Qh4** first.

7...	b6

Most books recommend **7...Nc6**, but the Black Queen Knight may be more useful on **d7**. By not blocking the **a8-h1** diagonal, Black hinders **e3-e4-e5**.

8 a4

With this, White serves notice that he will be watching both wings and has plans to develop his QN on **a3**. He may even expand on the Queenside with **Na3, c2-c3, Rb1** and **b2-b4!**

On the direct **8 Qh4** Black can defend with **8...Bb7 9 Nbd2, e6** and perhaps **...Nfd7**, e.g. **10 g4!?, Re8 11 g5, Nfd7 12 d4, Nc6!** (heading for *f5*) **13 c3, Ne7 14 Qf2, a6 15 h4, Nf5 16 h5, Rac8** as in **Pelikan-Maderna, Mar del Plata 1956.**

Another strategy for White is **8 Nbd2, Bb7 9 Bd1!?** with the idea of forcing **10 e4**. Black can play **9...Qc7** since **10 e4** will leave the f-pawn hanging. And on **10 Ne5** the retreat **10...Ne8!** favors Black (**Zita-Pachman, Czechoslovakia 1954**).

8...   Bb7

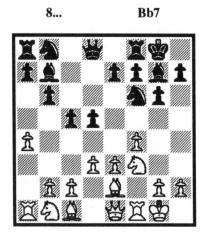

9 c3

Another prophylactic move. Again **9 Qh4** can be handled by **9...e6** and a later **...Nd7**. And **9 Nbd2** misplaces the Knight, e.g. **9...Nc6 10 Qh4, e6 11 Rf2, Nb4! 12 Ne1, Ne8 13 Qh3, Nd6 14 g4, f5** as in **Larsen-van Scheltinga, Beverwijk 1964.** With White's Queen on the Kingside the possibility of **...Nc6-b4** indicates that **9 c3** makes sense.

After the main line move **9 c3**, the move **9...Qc7**, despite **Na3-b5**, has been popular. In **Pelikan-Eliskases, Argentina 1955**, Black soon had the advantage in the center because of **9...Qc7 10 Qh4, e6 11 Nbd2, Nbd7**.

White seems to do better with the Queenside option: **9...Qc7 10 Na3, a6 11 Rb1** and then **11...Nbd7 12 b4, Ne8 13 Bd2, Nd6 14 Qh4, Rae8 15 d4, c4 16 b5, a5** was **Huisl-Nicolaiczuk, West German Championship 1978**. Both sides have ample play.

NOTES

NOTES

NOTES

NOTES

NOTES